WATERMELONS NOT WAR!

A Support Book
For Parenting in the Nuclear Age

Treat the earth well;
it was not given to you by your parents.
It was loaned to you by your children.

Watermelons Not War

A SUPPORT BOOK
FOR PARENTING IN THE NUCLEAR AGE

by Kate Cloud • Ellie Deegan • Alice Evans •
Hayat Imam • and Barbara Signer
of the Nuclear Education Project

New Society Publishers

Cover design and illustrations by Alice Evans
Book design by Barbara Benton
Design Assistance by Dion Lerman

ISBN: 0-86571-032-5 Paperbound
0-86571-033-3 Hardbound
Printed in the United States

New Society Publishers is a project of New Society Educational
Foundation. Your tax-deductible contributions to the Foundation will
enable us to contiune to publish similar projects. Make checks payable
to New Society Educational Foundation.

New Society Publishers is a founding member of Coop America, a
national marketing cooperative, and a collective of Movement for a
New Society, a network of small groups working for fundamental
social change through nonviolent action. The opinions expressed herein
do not necessarily represent agreed-upon positions of either of these
organizations.

Permissions

"Nuclear Warfare" is reprinted with permission from Ivy Clift.
"I am a kid for peace" is reprinted with the permission of Noah Wright
and his mother, Carol Wright.
"Jonathan's letter" is reprinted with the permission of Jonathan and
his parents, Doug and Judy Weinstock.
"Peace Action at the Grassroots: The Cambridge Peace Education
Project", by Hap Tierney, is reprinted with permission from the
author.
The Women's Pentagon Action has granted permission to reprint an
excerpt of the WPA Statement.
The Letter to Parents on page 110 is reprinted with permission from
Lynette Tarkington.

This book is made possible, in part, by a grant from the Anna H.
and Elizabeth M. Chace Fund, and by loans from the Philadelphia
War Tax Resistance Fund and the Lehigh Valley War Tax Resistance
Fund.

Thank You

We are grateful to RESIST and the Haymarket Foundation for providing initial support for our project; their faith in us gave us confidence.

There are countless friends and loved ones to thank, especially: Thomas and Deidre Deegan, Patricia Moore, Christine Lord, Marilyn and Toshi Mochizuki, Nathan F. Moore, Sandra Legotti, Lois and Sam DeWitt, Gus Block, Don Weitzman, Wen-ti and Hsuan and Hui-min Tsen, Bonnie Wynekin, Ilene Hauck, Gordon Thompson, Pat Farrar, Jean and Alex Humez, Caryn Kauffman, Barbara Sachs, Joshua Cloud O'Brien, Richard Madison, David Molnar, Joseph Hunt, Maya and Taras Mauch, Carol Strickland, Rachel and Kira Signer, Anne Ashley, Phyllis Kornfeld, the Horwitt family, Paula Phipps, Paula Kinney, Carolyn Krimsky, Lynn Lazar, Carol Adhanom, Cathy Cevoli, Palmer & Dodge Associates, Melissa Everett, Ike Williams, Nina Huizinga, and the Sisters of Silkwood.

We would also like to thank all children everywhere for their spirit, love and optimism, and the people of past and present generations who have cared and worked for the life of the world.

About the Nuclear Education Project

The Nuclear Education Project is comprised of five women from greater Boston who came together as a group shortly after the accident at Three Mile Island. All five of them are mothers. It was this fact that brought them together—each of them had been catalyzed by the accident into thinking about the world in which they were rearing their children. Each was concerned as a parent about how to deal with the despair they felt as individuals, how to talk with their children about nuclear threats to the future, and most important, how to begin to transform the world into a safe and nurturing place for all children. At first, the group served primarily as a loving support for members as they dealt with their own despair. It soon evolved into more: a study group, and finally a book-writing collective. Convinced that most parents everywhere were as concerned as they, the NEP spent the next three and a half years writing and compiling this handbook. In the course of writing it, each of these women has overcome, to some degree, the debilitating effects of despair and come to believe in the restorative empowerment of action. This book is their action and their offer of support to other parents facing the same fears, sharing the same hopes.

Thomas Deegan

Barbara Signer, Kate Cloud, Alice Evans, Hayat Imam, Ellie Deegan

NEP Members

Alice Evans is a landscape sculptor who also keeps a city garden that includes fruit trees, berries, flowers and vegetables. She has lived and traveled outside of the U.S., with three years spent in Beirut, Lebanon. She is currently a member of the Cambridge Commission on Nuclear Disarmament and Peace Education.

Born in 1938 in Jersey City, Barbara Signer has lived in towns in 5 other states, including Los Alamos, New Mexico, and for a few years in France and England. She works in a library, and has been active in community and school affairs. "I enjoy my children, family, friends, garden and a good joke. And I want a world where future generations will no longer ask my own childhood question: 'If there's enough food, why doesn't everyone have enough to eat?' "

Hayat Imam was born in Bangladesh, and has lived in the Middle East, England and the United States. A student of Indian classical dance, she finds comfort and inspiration in music. Her spiritual orientation is a source of strength in her work with women in the U.S. and in Bangladesh, and in her work toward a peaceful, non-nuclear future.

Eleanor Mahar Deegan is a parent and wife, a human services professional, a feminist, writer and artist. Her essay in *The Mothers Book*, Houghton Miflin, 1981, "On Despair, Hope and Motherhood," is her personal account of the transformation she went through as a result of the birth of her daughter. She is handicapped and feels this fact gives her a special outlook on the world.

Kate Cloud grew up in a large family in the Midwest. She has been a waitress, factory assembler, piano teacher, cleaning woman and secretary, and is currently employed in children's services. The women's liberation movement, the teachings of black Americans and a visit to an Indian village in the mountains of Guatemala have deeply influenced her political understanding. "If you want peace, work for justice."

About "Watermelons Not War!"

Four kids and two moms made a game of thinking up these alphabet slogans during a Mother's Day Disarmament Rally in Boston, 1982. We decided to use one of their slogans for the title of our book, Watermelons Not War!

Apples not atom bombs

Bananas not bombs

Coconuts not catastrophe

Doughnuts not death

Eggplants not epidemics

Food not famine

Grapes not guns

Homes not hydrogen bombs

Jellybeans not junk

Kiwifruit not killing

Lollipops not lice

Melons not murder

Nuts not nukes

Oranges not orphans

Popsicles not prisons

Quinces not quarrels

Rainbows not radiation

Sweets not sickness

Tangerines not tanks

United Nations not ultra-catastrophe

Vines not violence

Watermelons not war

Xylophones not x-tinction

Yaks not yes-men

Zebras not a zero world

Contents

Introduction

I can remember thinking about the state of the world before my daughter was born and feeling that I was powerless anyway, and that I might as well enjoy my life, or what was left of it. I admired people who put their lives on the line to protest. But there was no way I could picture myself as one of them.

The birth of my daughter changed all that. When she was only two weeks old, a nuclear cloud from the People's Republic of China found its way to our city and rained poison for two days. The fallout from a Chinese bomb test was contaminating my baby, and I knew I could no longer sit back and let others work for an end to this madness.

The accident at Three Mile Island happened when my daughter was two. Our television screen brought the image of anxious parents rushing their terrified children away from a deadly and invisible poison—radioactive fallout. I knew it might be me next time, snatching up my daughter in a daze of fear.

Now, when I hear about the Native American children playing on piles of radioactive rubble in the Southwest, or read about the mutated, cancerous children in Utah and Love Canal, it affects me nearly as deeply as if it were my own children.

I can no longer pretend that it doesn't matter because it hasn't yet happened to me.
Ellie

A Question of Power

We are five women who began meeting shortly after the accident at Three Mile Island, in the spring of 1979. We came together to talk about our hopes and fears for our children in an age of growing nuclear terror and uncertainty. We wanted to learn more about radioactivity and how it affects our children's lives. We wanted to find ways to answer our children's soul-shaking questions about the world. And we wanted to reach out to others who might be feeling the same way.

When we met, our children (eight of them altogether) ranged in age from three to nine. Some of us are single parents. One of us is physically handicapped. One of us, from Bangladesh, brought a Third World perspective to the group. We found that our common concern—the safety of our children in this nuclear world and our own need for support as we faced the problem—allowed us to appreciate and use our differences to enhance our mutual understanding.

4

The first few times we got together, we spent a lot of time just pouring out our fears and confusion and anger. We were struggling to face the truth about the world in which we were asking our children to grow and thrive.

One of the first things we did as a group was to write down our memories of growing up in the nuclear age. The process of dredging up those deeply buried memories brought back flashes of childhood terrors and secret fears.

Being very small. Dark green shades pulled down certain times of day. Bells ringing suddenly and twenty-eight children hiding under their desks, trooping down to the school basement. Thinking it looked like the war pictures I had seen in Life magazine. Ads on the still-new first TV, warning us of something called atomic attack. Films of burly men in hardhats waving people into tunnels and cellars. Black-and-white images of puffy, pretty clouds sprouting in the desert. Blood-red, sun-gold bombs blasting out of "our boys'" planes at Saturday afternoon matinees. Sometimes I tried to think about it. Usually at nap times or before I fell asleep at night. There was something called the atomic bomb. It was what made those puffy clouds. It was much worse than dynamite. It could melt people down. It could blow them to smithereens. We had dropped it on the Japanese because we had to. I had seen pictures of the children in Life magazine. I couldn't understand why we'd had to bomb them. I'd look at my favorite doll and I'd try to imagine her arms and legs flying off. I couldn't see how they would—she was all plump and smooth, without cracks that could be pulled apart. Then I'd look at my arms and decide that I'd be safe too. But I knew we could both burn (I'd seen pictures) and that worried me.

Writing down our memories reminded us how desperately we had wanted reassurances from the adults in our lives.

When I first learned about The Bomb, I was five or six years old, in the early fifties. I heard on TV that it could blow up the world! I was very worried about that, but my mother said the president wouldn't let anything happen to us. I tried to tell myself that maybe everything really was all right, and that the situation just seemed out of control because I was a kid and couldn't understand adult mysteries. But I kept thinking that the grown-ups weren't taking it seriously enough.

In the sixth grade they began to show us the movies. About energy and oil and coal and something called the peacetime use of atomic power. I was so relieved! My friend the atom. If they could use it for making energy, then they wouldn't have to use it for bombs. Yay! I could rest easier.

Almost without realizing it, our memories sometimes led us into the now, to thinking about our own children and our responsibilities to them.

As a child myself, the first intimations of disaster came when I was eleven or twelve years old. I was then living in Iraq, and the Suez crisis erupted. The air was thick with fear of a nuclear confrontation between the Russians and the U.S. It wasn't conversations or specific knowledge that helped inform my brother and me. Rather, the fearful aspect was the heavy silence of the adults on this subject. But there was enough awareness to cause a deep dread in the hearts of all the children. It was at this time that I started having apocalyptic dreams of the world ending. I still remember the impression of those dreams. . . . Perhaps the chill will never leave me and is still lodged somewhere in my being. . . . I have grown to accept my own death with a fair amount of equanimity, but everything ending is a different measure of despair. If we are not actively fighting to change things today, then we will have failed our responsibility to our fragrant children.

Talking about our memories and sharing our deepest fears and feelings about the world had some interesting results. Each of us in her own way began to alternate between despair and relief—despair over the enormity of the problem, and relief at finally being able to talk about that despair. We expressed our grief and guilt about the world we are offering our children, and we were strengthened and comforted by the knowledge that each of us was experiencing those feelings. Sharing our sorrow and outrage helped us to move beyond those feelings toward taking action.

Our children's trust and boundless optimism inspired us. We wanted to be worthy of that trust. And we wanted to respond with care and sensitivity to our children's concerns about their world and their future.

What is it like to be a child in the nuclear age? What are some of the fears children speak of and just as important, do not speak about? How can we tell them the truth about the world without frightening them? What are the social myths that burden them and what new myths can we give them?

We decided to write a handbook which could be used as a resource for parents, teachers, and those who work with children. We talked

with others about our ideas for this project, and we were astounded by the positive response we received. People from all over the country began to contact us. We began to feel a sense of community; we became aware of ourselves as part of a growing movement toward peace and reverence for life.

We've been motivated to write this book not only by our intense feelings of fear and dread, but also by our conviction that there are practical ways out of the present global dilemma. The political ideas and action suggestions we present reflect our own beliefs about power and responsibility. Not everyone will agree with our analysis or emphasis, and we welcome your criticisms. We offer our point of view, not as THE ANSWER, but as our contribution to the dialogue.

Above all, with this handbook, we want to reach out to each reader and say: You are not alone and you are not powerless. Working together, breaking through the isolation, children and parents and all caring people can turn things around.

Why are we destroying our life-support system? Why do we saturate the land, air, and water with poisonous substances that threaten our existence? How can we reverse this process?

These are questions we have asked ourselves many times as we worked on this handbook. We gave ourselves topics for study, and came back together to discuss what we had learned. We looked at how most of society had encouraged us to turn our attention away from the ever-growing stockpiles of nuclear weapons. We talked angrily of leaders who chat about megadeaths over lunchtime martinis.

None of us in the Nuclear Education Project is an expert. We knew very little about nuclear technologies (besides the fact that they were terribly dangerous) before we came together as a group. At first, with the accident at Three Mile Island so fresh and vivid in our minds, we focused our study on nuclear power. Soon, as we read and thought and shared what we were learning, we saw more clearly how everything is indeed connected. We could not understand nuclear power without also talking about nuclear weapons and the politics of energy. It became obvious to us, in fact, that we could not even confine ourselves to nuclear technologies. We realized that we were dealing with a life-denying system of profit and power, held in place by violence and intimidation.

How can we begin to transform such a system?

One of the most powerful tools we have at our disposal is actually a way of looking at things. It is seeing things in relation to the whole. Ecologists tell us that all natural systems are related and interdependent. Stresses and imbalances in any part of the web of life affect the other parts.

The same is true for social and political systems. When a small group claims ownership of most of the world's resources, the rest of us experience shortages. When only a few are deciding life and death issues for the many, the results do not reflect the collective wisdom and will of the majority of the people.

Those who control society's wealth and power and access to information would like us to believe differently. Their success depends on their ability to convince us that they are acting in our interests. They do not want us to understand the relationship between nuclear power and nuclear weapons. They do not want us to connect the mushrooming military spending plan with budget cuts in human services and social programs. They certainly don't want us to understand how racism and sexism and the exploitation of Third World peoples insure their profits.

It serves the interests of the powers that be to divide us by race, sex, nationality, income level—to have us oppose each other instead of them. When we are fighting among ourselves, then nobody's paying attention to the power plant down the road, the chemical dump next door, the strip mine a few states over.

We realized that one of the most revolutionary actions we could take was to stop trusting the leaders who defend the system and start believing our own perceptions.

After years and years of powerful programming to accept the explanations of the officials and the experts, trusting ourselves is no easy task. The experts put a great deal of effort and money into manipulating "the masses" (us). They have the media, the financial connections, and all the power of the system behind them. Through that system they tell us what to believe, what is right and wrong, what is necessary to protect the country, what is the most "patriotic" response to a problem. Through that system, they define sanity and rationality themselves, so of course they look sane and appear rational. And most of us, deep inside, want to believe them. It takes a lot of courage to admit even to ourselves that the twisted logic of greed and domination stands between us and our survival. It's awfully scary to be the kid who knows the emperor isn't wearing any clothes.

One of the best ways to begin to trust ourselves is to pay attention to the signals our bodies send out when we are being lied to. When our palms begin to sweat, it could be because we're being backed into a corner. When the muscles in our shoulders and the backs of our necks get tight, it's because we're trying to sort out the differences between what we know in our hearts to be true and what we are being asked to believe.

Sharing our perceptions with others is a good way to practice trusting ourselves. Most often we find that others have been thinking along the same lines. As long as we stay locked up inside our fears, we remain ripe for victimization. By talking about our feelings, our doubts and mistrusts, we can give ourselves and each other permission to doubt, to question authority. "Why?" is a powerful question, and it gets easier to ask the more we ask it.

I. The Heart of the Matter

Parenting For Possibility

As parents raising children in the last part of the twentieth century, we have more than enough to do. We care for our children in a world of economic strain, immediate neighborhood violence, racial and sexual hatred. We work hard to shelter and nourish our children's bodies and minds. Yet it is not enough. Parenting within the possibility of human extinction demands new, creative responses from us. Parenting now means we must ourselves face and help our children to face the realities of the nuclear age.

Children sense the danger and they ask questions. "What does overkill mean?" "Why do countries fight?" "Mom, what would happen in a nuclear war?"

Can we give honest answers to our children's questions about the world without shattering their fragile sense of trust and security? How do we teach kids not to act on impulse, when at every moment their lives are threatened by a holocaust waiting to happen? How do we discourage our children from taking drugs to escape the pain we know they feel when they think about the future? How do we foster long-term values and goals in a world that might disappear in an afternoon?

These are the issues we face as parents in the nuclear age. We must protect our children and help them grow strong and whole and hopeful. We need to discover and share ways of parenting that recognize and satisfy our children's needs in this frightening world. Now we are called upon to re-examine our ways of living on this earth and the belief systems that have brought us here. If we are to reclaim our futures and the futures of our children and their children and their children's children, we must create new belief systems, devise new ways of living.

*Ellie: **Do your friends ever talk about this stuff?***
(nuclear war, power plant accidents, etc.)
*Nathan, aged twelve: **No, never.***
*Ellie: **Do you worry about it?***
*Nathan: **Sometimes.** (His face is solemn. He won't look at me.)*
There is a pause. I try to be careful.
*Ellie: **How long have you known about this stuff?** (Neither of us has really named it. This conversation is not fun.)*
*Nathan: (Looking at the TV, not me.) **Forever.***

*Hsuan, aged nine: **News! It's so boring. Turn it off.***
*Alice: **Why is it boring?** (The newscast was a listing of the wars around the world.)*
*Hsuan: **I don't know. It's just boring.***
*Alice: **Is it all the bad news?***
*Hsuan: **Yeah. It's all the wars—the news is just full of wars. I don't want to hear it.***

Do Children Know?

In Boston there is going to be a war and there is going to be fire coming to earth. And from the sky a bomb is coming to earth. And the earth is going to split open. And fire is going to come down to earth. And my mother heard it on the radio and she told me and I heard her.

Third-grade child

Kids know the truth about our precarious situation. Deeply disturbing images pour out of the media and into our children's psyches in the same way that the terrible pollutants of this technological age stream into their bodies and their brains.

Newsbreaks interrupt Saturday morning cartoons with the latest updates on the arms race; mushroom-shaped clouds blossom between segments of *Wild World of Animals*, advertising the Public Broadcasting System's next special on the nuclear threat; images of Armageddon adorn the covers of national magazines, unavoidable as we stand in the checkout line at the supermarket. Unless we find a way to hermetically seal our kids off, nuclear issues impose themselves on them from every direction.

My husband's aunt confided in me one afternoon at a family picnic that she and her husband were deeply shocked to find out from their grown daughters that, as children, they had lived in fear of a nuclear war. Both my husband's aunt and uncle had assumed that since the girls never spoke of it, they hadn't known or been afraid.

Ellie

It is difficult for parents to think about children knowing all of this. We prefer to believe that they stay untouched by nuclear nightmares. But there is growing evidence that this is not the case, and that our children's young lives are being affected more and more as the nuclear menace grows.

What's Happening to our Children?

Children growing up in a world held hostage by nuclear terror show very particular kinds of developmental problems. "What work has been done demonstrates that children are aware of the threat of nuclear war and live in fear of it," says Dr. John Mack, Pulitzer prize-winning professor of psychiatry at Harvard Medical School. Dr. Mack helped conduct a study on the psychological and emotional impact of the nuclear arms race on adolescents attending high school in the greater Boston area. The findings confirm that children today are deeply troubled by a world that can't guarantee them a future.[1]

Questionaires were distributed to about one hundred adolescents in the tenth to twelfth grades. Based on the responses, Dr. Mack concludes:

We may be seeing that growing up in a world dominated by the threat of imminent nuclear destruction is having an impact on the structure of personality itself. . . . It seems that these young people are growing up without the ability to form stable ideas, or the sense of continuity upon which the development of stable personality structure and the formation of serviceable ideals depend. We may find that we are raising generations of young people without a basis for making long-term commitments, who are given over, of necessity, to doctrines of impulsiveness and immediacy in their personal relationships or choice of behaviors and activity. At the very least, these young people need an opportunity to learn about and participate in decisions on matters which affect their lives so critically.[2]

The teenagers' responses revealed their sense of menace and dread. They have trouble thinking ahead, and some have doubts about planning families. According to Mack, "There is also cynicism, sadness, bitterness and a sense of helplessness. They feel unprotected."

"It all seems crazy."

Our children see the craziness, the absurdity of the arms race. Like the kid in the fairy tale who loudly proclaimed, "The emperor is naked!", today's child sees right through the hypocrisy of praying for peace while preparing for war. And they look to us—the adults in their lives, their parents, teachers, grown-up friends—for some help in making sense of it all.

NUCLEAR WARFARE

It seems to me a trifle strange
That we may pray for peace
  And still build weapons.
If Utopia has no wars at all,
And we seem to seek perfection,
  Why must we fight?
Killing people has no excuse
Or none that sounds all right;
  It all seems crazy.
Russia and U.S. always fight
Europe can see her death
  WHAT IS THE POINT!
Ivy Clift
grade seven

What do children need?
Deidre, Six years old: Clothes, warm for the winter. Food, warm cereals for the morning. Lots of love. Water, juices, sleep.

What don't children need?
Deidre: War—guns, knives, swords. And they don't need to play with lightbulbs in the bathtub.

Children's innocence and hopefulness are precious to us. We don't want them to feel frightened, or to grow cynical. For most adults, the thought of children in danger brings up powerful protective feelings. We don't want them to be hurt. But today, in the nuclear age, all children are threatened. As we write this, it is now clear to most people that a nuclear war could destroy our world.

When a three-year-old imagines a monster under her bed, we can show her she has nothing to fear. But children's fears of mushroom clouds and firestorms are based on reality. Unlike the ordinary childhood fears of the dark or of monsters, they don't go away in the morning.

Apocalypse isn't necessarily so.
John Lennon, Parent.

How can we help our children who are growing up right now with the "secret" knowledge that they may never live to grow up?

There is still time to turn things around. We can give our children a great gift—the gift of hope. But we can only offer hope when we feel it within ourselves.

Most parents identify very closely with the vulnerability of their children. After the birth of a child, parents feel a deep urge to ensure the survival of the frail, miraculous new being in their care.

These powerful feelings of love and protectiveness make it difficult for us to confront the reality of today's nuclear terror. Many parents, especially those with young children, feel anxious and heartsick when they think about nuclear issues. Such thoughts often stir up a resurgence of their own childhood fears and insecurities. It is not unusual for parents to feel guilty for bringing new life into this world. We must try to let go of guilt and worry, because they wear us down and change nothing.

Find support in your community, be it a good friend or a parent group. Start a group of your own—but get support. Such support allows us to share feelings and work through our own despair.

> *The support of our group helped me to confront a lot of my fears. Now I'm not as afraid of my child's fears as I was when mine were all locked up inside of me. Kids sense your fears, and it makes them uncomfortable. I think an anxious silence can be far more frightening to a child than discussing the most horrific facts with a calm and loving adult.*
>
> *In our group, we shared experiences, swapped stories and brainstormed together. This kind of support has helped me to feel ready and present for my child. It's helping me to set up an atmosphere in our home where she feels permission to talk about her fears, ask questions, share insights.*
>
> Ellie

Our lives change when we begin to face these issues with the support and validation and love of others. We find that the energy that was stored up before releases itself. Our children hear us talking, see us acting and begin to gain courage. Now, more than ever, children need our encouragement. They need to know that adults are concerned about the world, and intend to do something about it.

There are many ways we can show children that we believe in the future. One of the most important ways is having the courage to talk with our kids about the threat to their world. In our group meetings over the past three years, we spent a lot of time sharing conversations we've had with our own children. These discussions highlighted the difficulty of writing about "how to talk to kids about these things." Each child is an individual, with unique experiences and questions.

We can help children sort through their feelings if we see that their questions are often conversation-openers. Often it's hard to know what the child is looking for from the questions, and so it is difficult to know how to answer. Turning the questions around ("What do you think?") can give us a chance to hear more from the child, and help us to know more precisely what the child's needs are at that moment.

Remembering always that "apocalypse isn't necessarily so" helps keep us steady as we grow with our kids in this extraordinary age. Children need to be reminded frequently that there are many, many people working for peace and real security. We know the media doesn't always report the good stuff as consistently as it does the bad. (The June 12th rally in New York—the largest disarmament demonstration in the history of the country—didn't make the cover of any of the big national magazines!) Our children need us to talk with them about the good stuff.

Of course, we can't talk about the movement towards peace without referring to the movement towards war. It's unavoidable, and it's never easy. But we don't have to have all the answers. Our children don't need us to have all the answers. Above all, we have to be there for them, and help them in working through their feelings, trusting their instincts, understanding connections, learning to hope, learning to love.

Nuclear realizations come to children gradually as they grow toward adulthood. When we discuss nuclear issues with our children, we can be guided by their age, their emotional maturity, and their unique place in the developmental process. We respond as individuals, with our own understandings and hangups. Often we find that the answer which comforts one child is not at all appropriate for another. There are no sure-thing prescriptions or magic words that will work every time. Helping to guide children through the maze of nuclear uncertainties is a living, creative process. With these thoughts in mind, we offer some suggestions that we found helpful.

You'll always be my mommy, won't you? Even when we're dead . . . we're all related, aren't we? Didn't we all come from the same parents, so aren't we all brothers and sisters? . . . Why do we kill animals? They're people, just like us . . . We're always doing something, aren't we? Even when we're dead . . .

These questions, asked over a period of time, were part of six-year-old Hui Min's attempt to grasp relationship and connectedness. Part of living is coming to terms with the fact of our own death. Most children will ask questions about death and existence at some point.

As they grow up, they try to understand their relationship to other people, to animals and plants, to all that is. Today, these natural questions may be prompted by a sense of dread, as children contemplate the ominous prospect of the death of the world.

We can find some guidelines for talking about nuclear issues at home from our experiences talking with kids about sex and death, or any other emotionally charged subject. We know we need to be age-appropriate and give them only as much information as they are able to handle. We have to be sensitive to the signals children give out when they have had enough: glazed eyes, fidgeting, interruptions to change the subject.

We don't have to set arbitrary times for such conversations. They'll come when the time is right. When nuclear issues do come up, we need to be very selective about what sorts of information we give to children. Hard nuclear numbers are terrifying and incomprehensible even to adults. There is no need for parents to give out this kind of information unless a child specifically asks for it.

No matter what questions children ask, we need to be able both to acknowledge for them the fearfulness of the situation *and* to reassure them. The acknowledgement of fear prevents the child from feeling crazy and alone. The reassurance gives them permission to feel that they don't have to *worry* about it. When our children hear our calm concern, they feel protected. When they see us caring, and willing to join hands with them in facing the fear, they are freed up to go ahead and be kids.

It reassured my kids when I simply said, "That worries me too." Kids are so practical, so egotistical. They really are centered on their survival, and frightened if their parents don't seem to be.

Barbara

Little Children: Ages 3—6

Little children, from three to about six, are usually oblivious to the nuclear threat. That's fine. Sometimes, however, even very young children seem to have flashes of it, especially if they are growing up in activist homes. These momentary awarenesses can be dealt with in big, warm generalizations: "War is bad. Many people get killed. But lots of us are working to stop all wars." There's no reason to tell small children horrible facts. There is no need to go into detail. In general with this age-group we do our best parenting for peace by giving children experiences of connection with the earth (nature, growing plants), self-expression (the arts, being listened to), and self-worth (praise, lots of hugs and kisses). We can help them experience themselves as important by asking their opinions on many subjects, and training ourselves to really listen to their responses.

One summer evening when my daughter was only three, we were in the bathroom together, going through the before-bed ritual. She was exceptionally quiet, I thought. All of a sudden she started to giggle, a really forced giggle. Then she said, "Judy says the world's going to die," (Judy was her four year old cousin) and giggled strangely again. I panicked for a couple seconds, and then, thanks to the months of support and preparation I had gotten from our group, I was able to respond without avoiding. "Honey," I said to the intense little face, "lots of people all over the world are working very hard to make sure that doesn't happen." She smiled a real smile and toddled off to bed, a three year old again, with a three year old's worries and hopes, not the weight of the world on those tiny shoulders.

Ellie

Older Children: Ages 6—8

Between the ages of six and eight, kids seem to make a big leap in comprehension. They begin to develop the kinds of skills (reading, following narratives, simple math, memory) that enable them to put information together and to draw conclusions. They are beginning to understand cause and effect and to really experience themselves as separate people. Because they are developing a self, an ego, they can begin to imagine death and non-existence in a more real, concrete way. It is at this age that children today are beginning to say quite sophisticated things about the nuclear world they live in. Some of them are already worrying about having kids. Many of them worry more about surviving than they do about dying. It terrifies them that they might survive alone.

Kids at this age need a lot of reassurance. They need help in articulating their feelings. As they get older, they may hide their feelings more. Using your own discretion, you may want to take some initiative. Invite the child to go with you to a rally, or to gather signatures on a petition. Teach the child an anti-war song. Encourage him or her to draw a picture about what peace is.

Many parents with children in this age group become alarmed when their kids, especially boys, seem drawn to violent, war-like play. It is disturbing, certainly, when a child draws pictures of bombs bursting in air and wants guns for toys, but in order to understand what is going on, we need to keep a couple of things in mind. Children express their developmental needs in terms of their culture and use the images the culture provides as a way to communicate those needs. Children (and people in general) need adventure, challenge and the opportunity to experience these human feelings. It is only natural that our children absorb this reality and express it by playing in the culturally accepted militaristic way. Added to this dynamic is the need of young children to announce their presence in loud, physical ways, the normal "roughhouse" play of all young mammals. Many adult pacifists remember playing cowboys and Indians or various other war-like games when they were small, a reassurance for parents who are disturbed by the future implications of such aggressive activity. Placed in its cultural context, war play becomes much more understandable.

We need to make a real effort to help children recapture the spirit of adventure for what it is. There are challenging kinds of activities that are non-violent in nature and that require heroic and powerful responses from children, but not nearly enough. Physical outlets for energy—running, swimming, gymnastics, martial arts, for example, all provide both the challenge and the heroic postures children want, and they need not be unduly competitive in nature. An exciting series of "New Games" has been developed which is inventive, fun and non-competitive.[3]

Finally, we can help children in this age group to experience their personal power by encouraging them to participate in family decision-making, a skill they will need as they struggle to learn and grow up in this complex world.[4]

Pre-Adolescents: Ages 8—12

Children between eight and twelve are beginning to develop the ability to truly empathize with people and things other than themselves. They are developing social awareness and what could be called a "moral sense." They can understand the concept of planetary death as well as personal death. They begin to express, along with fear, deep sadness.

I think loss of innocence for a child comes with the awareness of nuclear weapons and what their use would mean. Actually, I tried to protect my children, when very young, from many hard facts about the world, but I really dreaded the day when that particular awareness would become a part of their lives. The summer when my older child was eight I had helped organize an event for August 6th, Hiroshima Day. Books and pamphlets had been left at my house and my daughter picked one of them up to read. The book was Barefoot Gen *and relates in comic-book form the events of that awful day at Hiroshima. I wanted to run across the room and grab the book out of her hands, but of course I couldn't do that. I left her to read and went outside to work in the garden. It was a nice day and all the windows were open and it wasn't very long before I heard hard sobbing from my child. What could I do? I went inside and put my arms around her and we cried together. She could not understand how people could do such a thing. I wanted to do something for her. I wanted to ease that sadness and shock. It happened that I was circulating petitions in our neighborhood for the Nuclear Freeze ·and I decided to take her around with me as I knocked on doors. As it turned out she went with me twice and I think it heartened her to see so many people ready to sign the petitions supporting the Freeze and to hear their comments. It actually did a lot to restore her faith in adults and she was able to let that immediate sorrow go.*

Alice

These children seem to need an extra dose of psychic protection. Start hiding the magazines with the scary covers. This is a very imaginative age-group. Kids this age really need us to tell them a lot about the good news (the Freeze movement, for instance).

While working on this handbook I decided to interview my children. I asked my seven-year-old son Taras if he ever thought about nuclear power and radiation. He said; "I don't really think about it. When it comes into my mind, I think about good stuff like natural energy." My nine-year-old daughter replied: "I think radiation is terrible. I think about being dead. I try to keep my mind off of it. I try to think of nicer things. It's not hard to find nicer things!"

When questioned about what those nicer things included, she said; "I think of you, Mummy. You'll fix everything. You fix my bed. You fix Snoopy. You can make nuclear power go away." Rather overwhelmed, I asked her what made her think that. "It's because you do do it. I think you will succeed. I think of lots of people—mummys, daddys, kids, cousins, all saying no, no, no! We should have community windmills. You know, there's a law that if you can make extra power, you can sell it to the electric company. I saw it on TV." I asked her if she ever wanted information on radiation. Her reply was: "I really want to hear about the successes, not about dangers. I don't mind too much hearing how radiation is bad for you, but I don't like to hear about people getting k-i-l-l-e-d." Much energy was spent in their little heads avoiding scary information, which showed me that those ideas are there. I want to remember that my daughter wants gentle language when getting information. I am grateful that when those scary thoughts come to their minds, both kids have something positive to replace them with. But it also reminds me that in order to give them successes, we have to keep working.

Hayat

Children need us to listen to their ideas. Sometimes this can be pretty painful for the parent, but it is important to let the child feel his or her way through it. Their imaginations are there for the solutions to the problems as well as for imagining the horrors. Kids this age really see the absurdity of the nuclear mentality and they are usually pleased to communicate their insights. They often love to write letters and

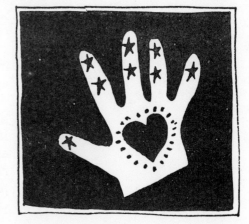

will drop a line or two off to the president with ease. Mailing the lettters and discussing the response, or lack of it, gives the child the experience of acting in the larger world.

Young Adolescents: Ages 12—15

Young adolescents (twelve to fifteen) are, of course, going through puberty, with all the stresses entailed in that experience. They are starting to know themselves as active, sexual creatures, and they are held tight by the social nature of their peer groups. Kids at this age may decide to tune out as much as possible from any kind of involvement with nuclear issues. If yours has been a family that has been active for a while, the early adolescent child may go through a period of rebelling against a parent's activism. Most parents who survive this stage say the kids usually come back when they're ready and on what they see as their own terms. Of course, this isn't always the case; some kids start to get very active at this age. At any rate, we must give them the freedom to be as involved or as uninvolved as they choose.

Adolescents realize they are becoming adults. They are often angry at their parents and at the world for willing them this mess. It is important that we respect their anger and their despair, and help them find their own ways of dealing with it. It's hard. Young adolescents are often very absolute in their moral judgments. Remaining flexible and loving and clear in our hope for their futures is the best thing we can do for them. Being honest about our fears and our experiences can only help them in the long run—even though they may act like they don't hear a thing.

Older Adolescents Ages 15—18

As adolescents get older (fifteen to eighteen), they will need a lot of practical help as well as moral support in making their early adult decisions. They are deciding how they will earn their livings, or whether to try school, about having families themselves. They may be experimenting with drugs or alcohol. They may be facing the draft.

We need to really encourage our young adults to listen to their inner voices, to find out for themselves, and to withstand societal pressures. But we must be prepared to accept their decisions when they have made them. We can be there for them when they ask us to be, but we must not try to impose our values on them. Taking them seriously, paying attention, loving them is the best we can do.

Our children's sense of trust and security has its roots in us and in our homes, no matter what the world is like. Values and goals grow and form in our homes, and our children learn primarily from us.

Parenting for peace in the nuclear age is a big task. But it doesn't have to be done all at once. It is a growing, long-term experience. It means for us a joining of hands with our kids as partners in struggle, and equally in celebration. The more we listen to our children, the more we learn. The more we love them, act for them, teach them about the world, the better we are preparing them to grow up in this complex culture with all its beauty and all its danger.

Remember, too, you don't always have to be talking about or acting on specifically nuclear issues to be preparing kids or to be doing something for peace in their lifetimes. Any time you fight to break down sexual stereotyping, teach new ways of conflict resolution, help a child to understand a new connection, you are working for peace. Confronting racism, sexism, classism—any form of "ism" that sets one group against another—in our homes, with our kids, is working for peace and preparing our children for the kind of world we must help them to build if war and life-threatening technologies are to be eliminated. Working for peace means working for justice and love, in our homes or in the larger world. Teaching our children to think creatively, imaginatively, and lovingly is working for peace. Helping them to find joy and pleasure in human difference—be it racial, sexual or spiritual—is working for peace.

San Francisco and Brookline, Massachusetts, among others, require that high-school students be provided with information on all aspects of draft registration, including alternative views to federal policies.

Through the efforts of parents and students, the Brookline School Committee passed a resolution stating that because "it is evident that allowing military recruitment and registration without presentation of alternative views is not in the best interest of Brookline students . . . appropriate informational materials, listing resources, speakers and community counseling groups should also be available to students, teachers, counselors and parents at Brookline High School."

Facing the Draft

We, as parents, feel a special responsibility to express our opposition to the current registration in preparation for a draft of the nation's youth. We are concerned not only for our own children and grandchildren, but also for all young people who might be ordered to kill and die for politics they did not make. Because registration and the draft represent military solutions to non-military problems, they increase world tensions and make war more likely.

from Parents Against the Draft's "Statement of Purpose"[5]

The Story of the Hundredth Monkey

The Japanese monkey, *Macaca fuscata*, has been observed in the wild for a period of over 30 years. In 1952, on the island of Koshima, scientists were providing monkeys with sweet potatoes dropped in the sand. The monkeys liked the taste of the raw sweet potatoes, but they found the dirt unpleasant.

An eighteen-month-old female named Imo found she could solve the problem by washing the potatoes in a nearby stream. She taught her mother this trick. Her playmates also learned this new way and taught their mothers, too.

This cultural innovation was gradually picked up by various monkeys before the eyes of the scientists.

Between 1952 and 1958, all the young monkeys learned to wash the sandy sweet potatoes to make them more palatable. Only the adults who imitated their children learned this social improvement. Other adults kept eating the dirty sweet potatoes.

Then something startling took place. In the autumn of 1958, a certain number of Koshima monkeys were washing sweet potatoes—the exact number isn't known. Let us suppose that when the sun rose one morning there were 99 monkeys on Koshima Island who had learned to wash their sweet potatoes. Let us further suppose that later that morning, the hundredth monkey learned to wash potatoes. THEN IT HAPPENED!

By that evening almost everyone in the tribe was washing sweet potatoes before eating them. The added energy of this hundredth monkey somehow created an ideological breakthrough!

But notice. The most surprising thing observed by these scientists was that the habit of washing sweet potatoes then spontaneously jumped over the sea—Colonies of monkeys on other islands and the mainland troop of monkeys at Takasakiyama began washing their sweet potatoes!

Thus, when a certain critical number achieves an awareness, this new awareness may be communicated from mind to mind. Although the exact number may vary, the Hundredth Monkey Phenomenon means that when only a limited number of people know of a new way, it may remain the consciousness property of these people. But there is a point at which if only one more person tunes-in to a new awareness, a field is strengthened so that this awareness reaches almost everyone! . . .

Your awareness is needed in saving the world from nuclear war. You may be the "Hundredth Monkey."[6]

Being involved in this work is deeply affecting the way I raise my children and my goals in life. Our work has inspired (and sometimes forced) me to consider what we face, and how I act has been changing profoundly.

The first time my children spoke to me about the threat we live with was not the first time it had entered our lives. Knowing, from my own experience and from reminiscing with friends, that awareness of the possible end of life on earth would come to my kids while they were young, I made sure they heard me say "nuclear power plants" and "atomic bomb" every six months or so, hoping that when the subject had meaning for Karen or Toby, they would feel comfortable discussing it. I was prepared for the questions, but not for the emotions. Their personal interest was triggered by the accident at the Three Mile Island electrical plant, and they were afraid.

"Yes, I'm upset about it too."

"Yes, it can hurt people, but it won't hurt you."

"No, you couldn't die from it." (I was beginning to lie.)

"Yes, we'll go stay with Aunt Sue in Buffalo if the wind blows our way." (Knowing I would probably stay put and make some excuse if it did.)

I was able to put away for later the pain of seeing their fear and the anger of knowing their spirits and bodies would continue to be threatened. The shocker was their anger toward me. I was a grown-up, I got to do what I wanted, so how come I'd let this plant be built?!

"But it was built before the danger was understood by most grown-ups, and don't you remember all the people who had put their names on my sheet of the petition to stop nuclear power, and the letter I'd written to the president?"

But they might get sick and there was pollution in the air, too, and I didn't care about their health because I smoked around them, and they were going out to play.

I lit a cigarette, began making dinner, and started to digest our conversation. How dare they be angry at me? I'm politically active when I think it may have an effect. I take care of them and love them, and go to work, and do it all over again—the childish myth of the all-powerful parent is a drag.

But they're right! My work is enjoyable and brings in the money that feeds us, but it's not going to improve our world any, and I do smoke. I have to accept that I do things that aren't good for them; I am part of the problem. And how have I lost that lively interest in self-preservation that's so automatic in childhood?

I realize that I can learn from my children.

At dinner I ask them how they heard about the accident, and after telling me (friends at school, who saw the news on TV or heard their parents talking about it), they mostly want to know if there's any way to protect ourselves. Thankful for my previous interest in the subject, I explain how we can drink lots of liquids

(unsugared), eat lots of fruit and green vegetables. (The scientists haven't figured out every reason why, but tests indicate this improves our resistance). Also, I tell them that by law, technicians all over America are monitoring the spread of dangerous emissions and we'll be told if any come to our region. Then I put them to bed in the regular way, and they go to sleep in the regular way. (Except Karen asks for two glasses of water.) After that day TMI seems to be mainly an exciting topic for my kids— like who was mean to who at recess. Karen writes her own letter to the president, they both drink a lot more water, want apples instead of cookies, and for several weeks prefer the security of their regular routine to anything new or different. We make an agreement that I will never smoke in their rooms or at meals.

For me, the relief of having "the subject" out in the open helped me to realize how much I needed to talk with other adults and find some group working to change our situation. The fantasy of a single individual changing everything wasn't going to help me change real life.

As our group came together, I experienced a bout of terrible anger at the now irrepressible knowledge that our country's wealth is being poured into technologies that are damaging, and may kill my children.

And I began to be aware of other angers, and sorrow. My children are being deprived. Systematically, and in every aspect of their lives, essentials I grew up taking for granted are being taken from them. Through the focus of this realization, all kinds of little things came together in an overwhelming lump.

My anger at all this was satisfying, the sorrow soothing. Once I had accepted how completely we are affected, my reaction was simple. I knew I didn't want this plastic life, and while supporting and working with others who were attacking specific problems, I turned to the treasures of the everyday.

I began watching my children and asking, "What do kids need?" "What's important to you?" My children talked about family and friends, work and play, a sense of security, and of not feeling alone. They wanted to know they would be taken care of no matter what else was going on, and to have people pay attention to them, even if they had to fight or act up some other way. They wanted to love, and be loved.

In NEP meetings we talked a lot about what makes life precious to us. When notice came of the demonstration in support of disarmament at the United Nations on June 12, 1982, I knew I needed to be there. I began making arrangements for my children to stay with relatives or friends. But Toby and Karen, now ten and eleven, said they wanted to go. "We want a future, Mom." I worried about money, and taking them into such a large crowd, but they had a wonderful time. It reassured them to see how many people cared, instead of just hearing about it. They were impressed to be part of those thousands of different people sharing a common determination.

So I was unprepared for a conversation that took place three months later. Toby and I were talking about whether we would rather have sons or daughters. Then I turned to Karen.

Barbara: What about you, Karen?
Karen: I'm not going to have any children.
Barbara: Why?
Karen: Even if I live to die a gentle death, I don't think my children could, so I'm not going to have any.
Barbara: What do you mean?
Karen: You know, there'll be a war with nuclear bombs, or too much pollution.
Barbara: I don't think so. So many people are working to change all that.
Karen: Well, I don't think they'll be enough, or be able to do it in time.
Barbara: How do you feel about that?
Karen: Sad.

As I write this, my eyes are filmed with fear, my heart feels cold, and I'm getting a headache from being so angry. Did I do this? Knowing from my own and other adults' memories what we felt as children, have I overburdened my children with facts, contributing to the fear and hopelessness I was trying to prevent? "When I grow up" is a different sort of dream for Karen. I had assumed my own reduced sense of life came from middle age and adult responsibilities. How could I give her a sense of hope? Did I dare to hope myself? Accepting the current situation felt easier than that. But I decided to give up the burden of thinking about what I didn't want, and start focusing on what I did want.

The idea of peace took on new meaning for me. We are living peaceful lives now. What is a peaceful life like? My kids said, "Being in the country and not being mean to each other, or taking more than my fair share." What were they learning that helped them live peacefully? "How to fight without hitting the other person," "taking turns; sharing; other people have rights too; maybe I can get it later; cooperating; saying what I want instead of taking it; having a nice day."

As we are talking more about peace in our NEP sessions, and as I have begun to notice what is peaceful in my day and in the lives of those around me, my feelings have changed. The sense of danger weighing on me and the thrill of fear that I experienced during the news come less often. I am beginning to feel more often the thrill of joy and sense of adventure I remember from my own childhood.

Yesterday, I asked Karen how she felt about having children now. She said, "When the time comes, I'll see how it is. I found that deciding things too much in advance gets me into a tight spot. If I'm going to be alive later, I have to live now, so I'd rather do that."

Barbara

How would you answer if your child asked:

"Why do people fight?"

Kate: (Just recently, Ned had a bright idea:) "Why can't everything be free? Why can't people just take what they need?" (He thought for a minute, and then his face fell.) "Oh, I guess some people would take more than they need, and there wouldn't be enough for the rest."

Why do people fight? They fight for a lot of reasons—to get what they want, to protect what they have, to dominate, etc.—but the first way I explained it to my child was simply greed, wanting to take for yourself more than you need.

Alice: Well, everybody fights. We all have angry and sometimes violent feelings. Depending on the situation we might discuss the cause—whether it's personal or international. We might imagine alternative scenarios to violence: how can this be settled via negotiations? What does each side actually need? Again, this is done for the Falkland Islands or the PLO/Israeli conflict or Hsuan and Hui-min screaming at each other. I might say vis-a-vis war that resorting to violence first is an old and habitual response but that many people are trying to find alternatives—that really we must find alternatives.

Hayat: I think people start a fight for two reasons. One is because they want to show that they are better than someone else; they want to prove their power. The other is because they are greedy and want something the other person has. You've seen yourself how easily children can get into arguments, trying to prove they are right about something that's not even very important. Grown-ups do that all the time. It's very hard for kids and grown-ups to admit they might be wrong and to give in to someone else's point of view instead of wanting to prove they are in the right. Kids also fight over things, a toy or something, and so do grown-ups. Entire countries, run by grown-ups, can get into war for the same reasons: to stay in power by insisting their point is the *only right one and because of greed over, let's say, resources like oil.*

But then there are fighters for the cause of good as well. These are people who usually don't start the fight, but fight back against injustice and cruelty. Unfortunately, things get complicated because each side always thinks they are the "good guys," the ones in the right, and pretends it's the other side that really started the fight. After awhile it's no longer easy to tell the "good guys" from the "bad guys." You've probably experienced that yourself when you've gotten into a fight with another kid and the fight itself becomes the problem. It almost doesn't matter any more who started it and what the reasons were behind it. Then it may become clear that finding another way to settle the argument would have been so much better. If it was because of wanting to be right, both kids could be considered "right," or if it was over a thing, some way of sharing or cooperating could have prevented the fight. Grown-ups and nations have to learn the exact same lessons, and because they haven't, the world has become a dangerous place to live.

Ellie: That's a hard one. Lots of people have been trying to understand that for a long time. There are lots of kinds of fighting. Sometimes you and I have arguments. Arguments are one way of fighting, and most people have arguments with other people. It's okay to argue, as long as we don't hit each other or say really mean things that we don't even really feel. I guess sometimes people don't know how to stop arguing. When countries argue, sometimes they have wars. Wars are a very complicated kind of arguing, and people kill each other. There are lots of reasons for wars, but most of the real reasons have to do with a very few people who have a lot of power and money. Those people will try to make us hate the people in the country that they want to fight. We need to remember that, in a war, everybody loses. We have to learn other ways of living so that we won't get involved in wars.

Actions in the Home

Working on this handbook has been a process of trying to understand nuclear issues and their larger connection in society, but it has also obliged us to turn inwards and scrutinize our personal behaviors and actions as well. In some ways, our homes are microcosms of society. Here we face issues of conflict, authority, and respect for each other. Here we vent our own frustrations and anger and also rejoice together as a family. It is also a place where we have the opportunity to give our children a foundation for their lives. There are no formulas or easy answers as we help them to achieve a sense of security, the right kinds of knowledge, and some control and power over their lives.

I asked my children how they thought home life affected their dealings with the world outside. Maya said, "Learning to talk over things with you and Daddy helps me to talk over things in school in an understanding way." Taras said, "There's one thing that really makes me feel bad, that's cleaning time, because you and Daddy scream at me—I think it's the tension—instead of just telling me what to do next time. We're all working, but people can make mistakes. If I go out right after someone yells at me, I feel really bad. If another kid came by, I would be rude. You kind of pass it on." This is my son, with his nine-year-old wisdom, teaching me how much care we need to exercise and how far-reaching are the effects of our mistakes in the home. While some days are better forgotten for their pettiness, others are rewarding for their possibilities. I would like to share some things that have worked for us as a family.

Above all my concern is to help my children feel safe in a very insecure world. I do this by giving them my unquestioning love and support, but more importantly by helping them to be aware of a greater love than mine, through a connection with God. I feel there is protection, and if they are open to it, they will feel protected as well. We talk about spirituality and pray together.

Another way to combat insecurity is to know we are not alone but part of a community of people who are in the struggle with us. When I hold meetings in my home, my children see other adults working for peace and sane energy and I think it is comforting to them. I have also noticed their eager enthusiasm whenever we have attended demonstrations and marches. We listen to a lot of music together. Songs widen their horizons and make them feel like they are part of a larger circle. At the same time, the impact of music with a message is astonishing! I watch them vibrate as a line in a song touches an innermost feeling.

I give my children reassurance and let them know the problems in the world are an adult responsibility; they do not need to take on the burden as children. Creating a climate where they feel comfortable bringing up things that worry them is important. I ask them indirectly if things are on their minds, and sometimes I ask them specific questions such as: "Are you worried about nuclear power?" Sometimes they answer me (some of these answers have been included in this handbook) and other times they give me clear signals they don't want to talk about it. They might ignore me completely or be more specific about their needs: "Sometimes I worry about it, but, right now I want to enjoy living without oxygen tanks and things like that while I can." (Maya, ten years old) I respect their signals because just as important as giving them permission to talk about things is giving them permission not to talk about them.

Our children gain knowledge in many different ways; it feels important to me to try to get involved in that process. We read together from favorite books. It's fun to make a "serial" out of a good novel like Jane Austen's Pride and Prejudice, and it also brings up opportunities for discussion of aspects of life-values

and morals. As a child, I remember being deeply influenced by characters in novels who displayed moral strength and courage! It's also good to monitor what children are reading on their own for content and age-appropriateness. This will depend upon our own instincts as parents. It helps me to remember how certain types of reading affected me as I was growing up.

Helping children to trust themselves begins by allowing them to gain some power and control over their own lives. When my children fight, hard as it is for me not to jump in (to ease the noise level alone!), I let them try to work it out for themselves. There are certain ground rules that are already set however, such as no hitting or name-calling. We have also discussed the issue of conflict together, knowing that conflict is a part of life and they will face it in and out of the home. I try to let them know that there is nothing wrong with conflict in itself: it is possible to disagree with one another without necessarily being hostile. In terms of dealing with conflict in the world, their own reactions in a conflict situation are ultimately the only things in their control. They may not be able to change other people's behavior—for example, they may not be able to stop another child from calling them a name—but they can be in charge of whether or not they react. This last point in particular is easier said than done, and may take a lifetime to learn. I know I am still struggling with it as an adult. But having talked about it, I find the children exceedingly responsive to the sense behind it.

When adult intervention is sought during a fight, I listen to each one and then make a judgment as to who was responsible. They are fair enough to accept that, but if the reaction is intense from one child, I know I've missed a point somewhere and I usually backtrack and try again. Children have a deep sense of justice that asks to be honored. Occasions on which they feel I have been unfair are long remembered, and yet they can accept strong limit-setting when it is just. One final point about children's fights is that when things are hot and heavy, a drink of water for each can do wonders to calm them down!   The issue of authority is one in which a sense of balance is critical. As parents, we have final responsibility for our children's well-being. I feel fine about exercising authority and expecting respect from them. At the same time, I respect their feelings and needs in the family. A family meeting can be called by anyone to air grievances and negotiate changes. Parents and children are reminded equally not to interrupt when someone is speaking. These steps are not really as formal as they sound. They are examples of a way of being which accommodates parental limit-setting with mutual respect.

Hayat

How would you answer if your child asked:

*What would happen
if there was
a nuclear war
and you were killed
and I was the only
one left?*

Kate: I don't know what would happen, but I suppose you would go and look for others. Then, when you found them, you would help each other. There are many fine and decent people in every part of the world and those who survive will try to help each other and make things better in the future.

Alice: **That thought makes me feel so sad, I don't want you to be alone; I love you so much. But I think there might be other people who can help take care of you. Don't you think someone would see you and say, "This child needs help"?** (What would come next? I don't know, but I'm sure the child would be snuggling in my lap.)

Hayat: **That's a very scary thought, I know. But even if I were killed, the chances are there would be other people there to look after you . . .**

Ellie: **Honey, if they drop the bomb here, we will all be killed. You won't survive and be left alone, I promise. We'll all be together forever and forever.** (What kind of world is it if this is reassurance?)

Barbara: **That couldn't happen. If you were alive, there would be other people too. What would you do?** (I see this question as wondering about autonomy and independence and growing up—one of many scenarios kids create when they're growing up.)

---

*"What can we do
to make the
world safe?"*

Kate: We can work for a peaceful world, starting with ourselves. We can take special care of the goodness within ourselves, and always try to respond to the goodness within others. We can join with others in groups devoted to peacemaking. We can make sure to tell our elected representatives how we feel about nuclear weapons and war. If they are not representing us well, we can work to elect people who will work for peace.

Alice: Love, faith, justice, ending hierarchies. "We have to care for each other very much. We have to decide that we will work for each other's good, that the well-being of everyone is a trust we take seriously. That means being conservative, using resources well, valuing life above everything."

Hayat: We should put pressure on all our governments and let them know we are watching them so they can't go ahead and do anything they want. We can do this by demonstrations, letters, by lots of people acting together. We can also pray for protection and align ourselves with the good "force." Most important, we should try not to get discouraged but keep remembering that we can make a difference. Be positive.

Ellie: There are lots of things we can do. Some things are right inside of ourselves, believe it or not. We can start by learning to be peaceful and happy in the world. It's good to like living, to like ourselves and to like other people. It's good to like the earth. It's not wrong to feel bad sometimes—that's part of being alive too! And it doesn't mean you have to like everybody you meet, only that you know in your heart that it's okay for those people to exist, even if you don't want to be with them. There is an old saying that I like to think about when I don't know what to do with my feelings: "Harm none, and do as you will." That means it's okay to do or feel anything as long as you don't hurt anyone or anything—including yourself, animals, plants, and other people.

Barbara: Take care of ourselves and the world and the living things around us. There are lots of ways. What would you like to do to make the world safe?

Kate: If it seemed likely that there would be a war soon, we would think about what to do. We might want to go visit David on the farm. We would talk to our friends and relatives, and then we would decide.

Alice: No, I don't think so, not if there is a nuclear war. That's why disarmament is so important. (I avoid this one, I must admit. It has never been asked directly. In fact, I always hope if there is a nuclear war that my children will die immediately, without suffering. I can't stand the thought of their goodness being violated so cruelly. I want them not to feel or know.)

Hayat: War can take so many forms it is difficult to know how it will be and what we should do. If it's a regular war and they tried to draft people, we would resist and do everything to prevent either of you from being drafted. We would claim exemptions as conscientious objectors (which means we don't believe in war to solve problems). If necessary we would leave the country. If it's a nuclear war, we will not have very many choices for safety. The only safety is to prevent a nuclear war, so we have to work very hard right now to make our feelings known to the government. At the same time we must pray for protection and put out positive energy from our souls to make a safe world. I really feel that the positive thinking of many, many people makes a difference. We must all join in—you, too.

Ellie: There's nothing we could do if there was a war. People can't run away from nuclear weapons. No place would be safe: radiation travels on the wind. All the big cities would be destroyed and there would be no help for people. What we do is stop a war before it gets started. We can work with all the other people—Mommies and Daddies and kids everywhere—who are working to prevent war to make the whole world a safe place.

Barbara: 1. Get together with other people and work to stop it. ("What if they gave a war and nobody came?")
2. Not really, if it's a big nuclear war. That's why it's important to get rid of nuclear weapons. You know, there are wars going on right now in the world.

"What are we going to do if there is a war? Is there any safe place to go?"

Dealing With Despair

Most of us were aware as children that there was something very terrifying in our world. It was then called "the atom bomb" or just simply "the bomb." Many of us remember "duck and cover" exercises at school. Some of us remember seeing magazine pictures of the people of Hiroshima and Nagasaki.

Many of us tried then to talk about these things with our parents and were met with a silence that spoke louder than words. We received the message loud and clear: talking about, even thinking about, the threat of nuclear disaster was a waste of time. These matters were best left to the leaders and there was nothing the average person could do about it in any case.

Why did so many of the important adults in our lives discourage our questions? We can speculate about the reasons for their silence. Perhaps they did not realize how totally the world had been changed by those first atomic explosions. Many were comforted by a faith in institutions that we today lack. They didn't know how to discuss such frightening new concepts with children. Whatever their reasons, most of us learned at an early age that we would not be encouraged to understand, talk about, or act on our fears of nuclear destruction.

As we grew up, most of us pushed those fears into the background. The Cuban missile crisis catapulted them to the front for a few immense days, and then it seemed we let ourselves for the most part "forget" again. Indeed, in order for us to grow up and start our adult lives, it may have been necessary for us to "forget."

But none of us has ever been able to truly, totally forget. As the twentieth century has worn on and the superpowers have built up huge nuclear armadas, we have all known somewhere deep within ourselves that our world is careening toward destruction.

Feeling powerless, most of us have struggled for years to contain our terror and to hold our awareness of the real situation at arm's length. We've developed ways, most of them unconscious, of screening out terrifying information and turning our attention to our individual lives. We've masked our insecurities with layers of day-to-day concerns. "I don't think about it," so many of us have said, slamming the door shut on discussion and action.

In doing so, however, we have paid a price. A generation of silence and avoidance has allowed the nuclear monster to grow unchecked. We are now finally being forced by history to look that monster in the eye.

When I first began to let myself really imagine what was meant by nuclear holocaust, I was overwhelmed. It was after my daughter was born. Somehow before that it didn't seem to matter so much to me. But holding her, so sweet and helpless in my arms, and realizing what could happen, I felt frozen with panic. Sometimes it would just sweep over me, out of nowhere. My chest would get all tight—I couldn't breathe. In my mind's eye I'd see houses blowing apart, trees bending first one way and then the other in what I knew was hot nuclear wind. Sometimes I couldn't move for minutes. When it passed, I'd cry and feel weak and furious. My baby, how could I protect my baby?

Ellie

Many of us experience deep emotional changes as we come to terms with the precarious world situation. At first, when our walls of resistance begin to crumble, we often try to shore them up. At this point our fears are closer and we are more conscious of pushing them out of our minds. We may use a great deal of energy, sometimes in frantic activity, trying to turn our awareness away. At the same time, we are apt to begin unconsciously to suppress other emotions too, since to feel joy is to risk facing the horror that could destroy it. We are prone at this stage to cynicism, despair and feelings of helplessness. We feel dulled and depressed and terribly alone—afraid to feel good, afraid to acknowledge our fear.

> *We sleepwalk through our lives, clinging desperately to the social warmths, the ordinary struggles, the private, personal parts of our lives. We close our eyes and we pray, but when we open them the threat is still there. Prayer won't do it. Pretending it isn't there won't do it.*
>
> *The reality of the situation is this: if we do nothing, we will die and our children will die. Perhaps existence itself will die. It is truly as simple as that. Those dear little bodies we have cuddled and spanked, sung to and yelled at, will never grow up to struggle themselves with what it is to parent and to love, to cry and to laugh.*
>
> *We try to pretend it isn't so, that somehow we'll all be safe. We are caught as people and as parents in a Catch-22: we can't hold the potential horror in our minds for long without feeling close to crazy, and yet to act like it's not there really is crazy.*
>
> Ellie

If at this point we can muster our courage and speak of our fears to others we trust, it is a great help. Right now, there are many people coming to terms with nuclear realities, and we can offer each other solace and support. This support is essential, for we are experiencing loss and grief—as real as any other loss and grief—but difficult to integrate since it is loss and grief about the future. When we first reach out and express our fears, we may feel overwhelmed by powerful emotions as our blocked feelings come pouring out. We may find ourselves temporarily obsessed with "nuclear nightmares." We must confront our deepest despair in order to get beyond it, to hope and positive action.

We do not magically leave fear and despair behind. But with love and support from each other, we can turn the energy of our powerful emotions toward survival. We can begin to think about how we can help to change the world.

Our new way of being in the nuclear world is marked by both despair (we may not succeed) and hope (we may change the world). We join hands with others and make the leap of faith: "I will love and feel. I will live as if the future were possible. I will work with others to build a world in which all children will grow up free of terror and despair." We have become adults in the nuclear age.

I refuse to accept the cynical notion that nation after nation must spiral down a militaristic stairway into the hell of nuclear destruction. I believe that unarmed truth and unconditional love will have the final word in reality.

Martin Luther King, Jr.
(speech accepting
Nobel peace prize,
December 11, 1964)

My "nuclear nightmares" began around the time my son was born. They were all incredibly vivid and three dimensional. When I'd wake up from one of these dreams, I felt sharply disoriented, as if I had been physically ripped from another world.

. . . I am walking through a gray landscape, passing large structures of metal, pipes, and towers for purposes I can't identify. There are no people or animals or plants, and there is an ominous bleakness about the scene. It is utterly silent and I am alone.

. . . The wind is blowing very hard, in unpredictable waves. People are clinging to trees and buildings, but everything is disintegrating or blowing apart. Things are flying through the air that shouldn't be there. There is no escape.

These dreams were associated in my mind with the threat of nuclear devastation, and with my helpless baby. I would wake up feeling terribly sad, anxious, and fiercely protective. Sometimes I would remember the dreams in great detail during the day, as I held my son.

The daily news was often deeply disturbing to me. Once I heard on the radio that a fire had released toxic fumes in a large cloud over Chicago. The officials were not sure if the gas would dissipate, or descend on the population. The image of an unpredictable poisonous cloud took over my mind and I began to shake. My husband wanted to know what was wrong. I told him I was cold but he said, "You're not shaking like that because you're cold." My body was wracked with terror.

I found that I was becoming a very fearful person, and I considered therapy. Finally I decided to work on the problem with myself. At quiet times during the day, I would gently ask myself what I was really afraid of, and pay attention to what came to mind. Before I went to sleep, I would suggest to myself that these dreams were my dreams, and I could take charge of them. I made an effort to be more conscious of myself during the nightmares, and to take action to change the situation within the dream itself. I also became more politically active, and started to learn more about theories of social change.

Gradually, I felt in control of my fears of world destruction and loss, and the nightmares left me. The fear is still there, but I have looked at it calmly and closely. Somehow that lonely self-examination helped me to rob the fear of its power to paralyze my energy. I'm not shaking in fear any more. Now I'm shaking the system that values death over life, hate over love.

Clare

Not long after Ronald Reagan was elected president, I had a dream which provided for me a really clear and poetic image for what I knew was going to be coming down on all of us from Washington during his administration. At that time, I was working as a teacher in a toddler day care center. This was the dream:

I walked into the big playroom at our day care center to find it devoid of children and staff. There was a large metal object sitting in the middle of the room and as I approached it, I suddenly realized what it was. It was a bomb—an old-fashioned(!) first generation nuclear weapon like the kind the U.S. had dropped on Hiroshima. I was beginning to feel really confused and scared when the head teacher, a super-efficient sort of woman whose motto always seemed to be 'don't rock the boat' walked into the room. 'What's this?' I asked her. 'Oh,' she answered in a casual, off-handed way, 'didn't you know? President Reagan has ordered one of these for every day care center in the country.'

Remembering the dream later, I was struck by how profoundly appropriate the image was, and moved again by the power of the unconscious to make simple and important connections in such a visual and powerful way.

Ellie

Despair in this nuclear age is never very far away. It overtakes me at unexpected times—in the movie theater with my husband and daughter, waiting for E.T. to start; leaning over my daughter to kiss her a safe goodnight. Action is a good antidote to despair, certainly, but no one is active all the time, and everybody gets tired.

Sometimes I am swept with "nuclear visions." I don't think I can go on working against it. It all feels too huge and too entrenched—completely unavoidable. Why not stop, I ask myself, and just go on with my life doing what I want and what I have to do? It is really disheartening to think that I've been working for peace for three and a half years and other people have been at it much longer than that and nothing substantial has come of all our hard work. In fact, there are more missiles, more bombs, more chance of devastation than ever. Sometimes I feel like I'd rather kill myself than continue with this horror.

But I don't. And I go on. I guess I'm becoming convinced in a really deep and permanent way that we—all of us—make the reality that we call the world. It is, after all, really up to us and we can prevent holocaust by wanting peace with all our hearts and souls. Our collective desire for world harmony will guide us in bringing it about. If I and other people just like me— ordinary, everyday folks—if we don't keep up our strength and hope, then the horror will happen. It will be inevitable. So I pick myself up, take a deep breath and make myself go on. The support and love of my friends and family give me strength, but it's never easy.

I wonder sometimes (and this may sound just a bit bizarre) if going through the whole thing psychically will somehow magically prevent it from actually coming to pass. Some psychics and mystics have said that we live a lot out in our dreams so that we don't have to go through the experience in our "real" lives. I hope that's true. I comfort myself that it is.

Understanding despair in this light helps me a lot. I can even begin to see beyond the possibility of holocaust into the kind of positive future we could weave for ourselves if we want it badly enough. As Jonathan Schell says in The Fate of the Earth, *ultimately all we have that stands between us and destruction is our love of life.*

When we first begin to struggle to face the nuclear threat, our struggle is to wake up out of the psychically numb state we have expended so much energy to construct. Later though, when we are facing it in all its horror, it becomes impossible to live in a constant state of awareness. At this point most of us find it necessary to "forget" again for most of our waking hours. And that's all right. In fact, this kind of numbing is what allows us to work and not go crazy. To hold the reality of possible holocaust in front of us at all times would be impossible, and not very productive even if it were possible.

Nora

Conversation

(Toby is eleven, Karen is twelve)

Toby: **You know, I don't mind if I die, I just don't want to die from nuclear war.**

Barbara: **I don't want it either. That's why I'm glad there's beginning to be more peace education.**

Toby: **What kind of peace education?**

Barbara: **All sorts . . .**

Toby: **I think if I die I'll go to hell, because my country made nuclear weapons and war.** *(She begins to cry. Karen, who has come into the kitchen, begins patting Toby on the back.)*

Barbara: *(making the juice)* **Well, we're working to stop it, and it won't go on if we can help it.**

Toby: *(angrily)* **I can't help; what can I do to help?**

Barbara: **We went to New York with all those other people from so many places, and you've written letters.**

Karen: *(putting bread in the toaster)* **The president never even reads those letters. He hires people to read them.**

Barbara: **It's our taxes that pay those people, and they're people too. And so many of us are writing letters that the leaders are beginning to have to pay attention. Toby, did you have a dream about this, or did something happen to remind you?**

Toby: **I don't need dreams to remind me.** *(They start eating breakfast.)*

Barbara: **Karen, does this worry you?**

Karen: **Of course it does, but what's going to happen is going to happen and I have to get on with my life.**

Toby: **You know, if a bomb did get fired, that doesn't mean you have to fire another bomb. See, if Russia fired a bomb on us, it would be terrible and millions of people would die, but if the U.S. didn't fire back, then people on the other side of the world would survive and could go on. I just thought of that** *(proudly).* **I'd feel better if I thought some life went on.**

Karen: People are the same everywhere, and someone would want revenge. Can I have some more juice?

Toby: Well, the ones who don't want revenge could stop them. They could disconnect the buttons, secretly.

(Karen leaves for crossing guard duty.)

Toby: If it did work out the way you hope and we gave up war, the bombs would still be here. Is there any way to get rid of them?

Barbara: There's an idea to put them in a package and send the package out to circle the sun, like a little planet.

Toby: I like that idea (smiling) "Put them in a package." But later, it will fall into the sun and the sun will blow up.

Barbara: Most of the stuff in the bomb has always been part of the solar system, and it's only if the nuclear reaction is set off that different stuff gets made. So if the package fell into the sun, it would just get mixed back in.

Toby: Oh, that's great. Venus could be habitable. If you take away the clouds it wouldn't be so hot. The clouds keep the heat in.

Barbara: Like insulation.

Toby: Yes, and the surface is fine to live on. I wish there really were superheroes. Because if a bomb did go off, they could just scoop it up and hurl it off into space. Remember how Superman did that in the movie?

Barbara: (laughing) Right! Where's the Greatest American Hero now when we really need him? It takes a lot of ordinary people to make the effect of one superhero.

Toby: I'm going to school now.

Barbara: Are you all right?

(Toby shrugs)

Barbara: I'll be thinking of you all day.

Toby: Well, bye Mom. Hope I'll see you soon.

Sometimes I feel as though I have to balance a whole culture: the fear, the despair, the violence. It's hard. At times my anxiety spills over but I don't give in to daily despair. We have to connect with each other—but I guess you have to connect with yourself first and figure out what you value and want. There are so many things I enjoy, and I don't want to be cheated of these pleasures by despair. I want my children to love and honor life, to be in terms of creative transformation, to care for people. So we celebrate quite a lot. We visit with family and friends. We plan and enjoy meals—we don't need much excuse to prepare something special. We read together in the evenings. We grow vegetables and flowers. We sing. We play games. I think that the children make larger connections and learn to honor life through our daily life. We don't make big conversations about it; we just do it. I think it's a good grounding for them.

My children are very trusting, and I feel I must deserve that trust and faith in me by being honest with them. When they do ask difficult questions about nuclear war, for instance, I don't give them false hopes. I don't say, "Everything will be all right." But I do tell them that people everywhere are working hard to stop wars and nuclear weapons. the children see the work that I do, and sometimes go with me to petition or attend a rally.

Faith in the future isn't a given. At this point, I will faith because I don't want to live without it, and because I feel it to be a responsibility. Faith can become real in this way, and that faith in our human society is felt by children. We all become stronger.

Alice

II. Nuclear Realities

Nuclear Power

In this chapter, we talk about nuclear power and the impact it has on our lives, our children's lives and the environment as a whole. We discuss the accident at Three Mile Island, and reactions to it—our own, our kids', TMI neighbors and others. We take a brief look at the basic physics and mechanics of nuclear power, at the fuel cycle, the waste problem and the politics of the nuclear industry.

This information aided us greatly in our understanding of the problem and helped us feel more competent when we discussed energy issues with our children or with other adults. This chapter is not a complete discussion of the nuclear industry, of the mechanics or the history of this most dangerous business. Rather, we see it as a first primer for parents, most of whom are probably as confused by the double-speak of industry and government officials as we were. For parents who would like to pursue the subject in depth, we have a good starting bibliography at the end of the book.

We hope that, after reading this chapter, parents will feel more capable of answering their children's questions about nuclear power and won't feel overwhelmed when a little voice queries, "Mommy, what's a meltdown?"

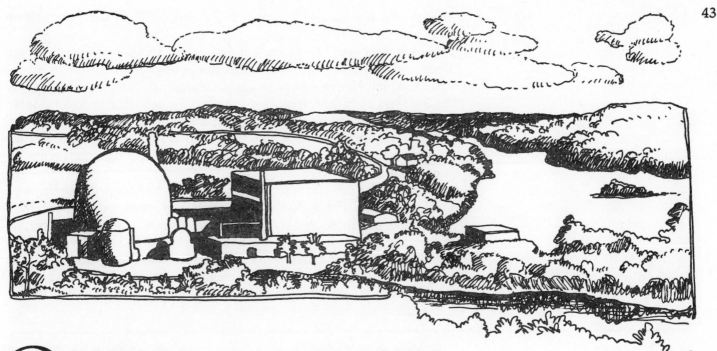

On March 28, 1979, the world looked on in horror as the Unit II reactor at Three Mile Island in Pennsylvania came within thirty to sixty minutes of a meltdown. For three days no one knew whether catastrophic amounts of radiation would be released into the atmosphere. The screaming headlines and our own fears made the accident a terrifying reality, bringing to our attention the whole issue of nuclear power. For the first time, many of us realized that this nation is dotted with nuclear power plants and that we faced the possibility of accidents like Three Mile Island happening twenty minutes from our own homes. "We all live in Pennsylvania" became a meaningful cry from Europe to California.

We were lucky at Three Mile Island. We were spared a "complete meltdown." With time, the urgency of those days has left us and the intense horror we felt has become a dim memory. The nuclear industry is counting on our short memories, but too much is at stake for us to forget the lessons of Three Mile Island. The fear we felt was justified. We were very close to a devastating accident in 1979, and it could happen again. We were betrayed by the nuclear industry's promises that a core meltdown could not occur. We should remember that when it nearly did happen, there were no apologies from the nuclear establishment. In fact, when we were miraculously spared the worst possible accident, the nuclear industry and its supporters took credit for it and pointed a proud finger at their safety systems!

But we are not the same now as we were before the accident. It is now more difficult to believe in the myths of our society that tell us the scientists know what's best for us and that technology has all the answers. We remember that the scientists were baffled and the failsafe technology nearly failed at TMI.

This chapter is designed to help us understand concepts of nuclear power by placing it in the context of the accident at Three Mile Island. Presently, public attention is focused on the urgent issue of nuclear weapons, but nuclear power is still a problem and will continue to be a problem in the future.

In fact, in many ways nuclear power and nuclear weapons are two sides of the same coin. Both industries pose grave radiation hazards; both exploit Native American lands for uranium; both create enormous quantities of radioactive waste; and, most sobering, nuclear power plants produce a by-product—plutonium—which is a key ingredient in the manufacture of a nuclear bomb. Every nation that has an average-size nuclear power plant can collect enough plutonium to create a nuclear weapon.

The media can create or "uncreate" issues by broadcasting them or ignoring them. But decisions about nuclear weapons and nuclear power affect all our lives, and the lives of future generations, so deeply that we must keep it in front focus whether the media chooses to or not. We may not read much about Three Mile Island any more, but it is still affecting people in Pennsylvania. And whether or not nuclear power is highlighted by the media, it remains an enormous problem for the entire world.

What is a nuclear power plant?

Most power plants—oil, coal, or nuclear—operate on the same principle: creating heat to boil water. The boiling water turns to steam, which is carried to a generator. The steam spins the generator to produce electricity. In a nuclear power plant, the fuel used is a metal called uranium.

The most important component of a nuclear power plant is the *nuclear reactor*. In the core of the reactor, there are bundles of long, thin rods filled with uranium fuel. Uranium does not burn like coal or oil to produce heat. Heat is produced in the reactor core by splitting uranium atoms, a process known as fission.

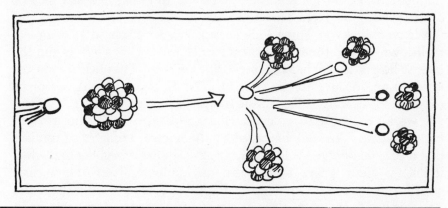

How does splitting atoms produce heat?

All matter is made up of *atoms*. Atoms are very tiny—so tiny that millions of atoms could fit into this dot. Each atom has a *nucleus* at its center which consists of protons (which have positive electrical charges) and neutrons (no charges). The nucleus is surrounded by orbital electrons (negative charges) that whiz around so fast they seem to blur into a sort of cloud or shell around the nucleus. The number of protons in an atom gives us the *atomic number* of an element.

The nucleus of the atom holds the key to nuclear energy. The protons and neutrons are packed together very tightly and hold a huge amount of energy. The energy that holds the nucleus together is unlocked by splitting the nucleus of the atom, and is then released in another form of energy: heat.

How Does One Split an Atom in the Nuclear Reactor?

Atoms of uranium are split in the reactor by sending a neutron into the nucleus. The nucleus then breaks up into fission fragments, releasing heat and more neutrons. The free neutrons then collide with and split other uranium atoms, causing additional heat and releasing still more neutrons that go on to split other atoms. This is called a chain reaction.

In an operating reactor, millions of uranium atoms are splitting at any moment, generating tremendous heat. This heat boils water and turns it to steam, which the turbine generator uses to produce electricity.

When I first heard about nuclear power, I had this image that when atoms are split, somehow electricity pours our of it! It gave me such a shock to realize that the awesome technology of nuclear power is just a way to boil water. This really is overkill!

Hayat

What is a Meltdown?

When the chain reaction is going on in the reactor core, tremendously high temperatures are reached. It is essential that there be some means of preventing this heat from going out of control.

The nuclear industry relies on two methods to prevent a dangerous rise of temperature. One is to insert *control rods* into the reactor core to stop the fission process. The control rods act like blotters to soak up the free-moving neutrons so that the chain reaction is stopped.

The other is to cover the hot reactor core, at all times, with cooling water to carry off the heat. If for any reason there is a loss of this cooling water and the water drops below the level of the fuel rods, the rods become so hot that they melt. This then is a meltdown, when the whole mass of incredibly hot uranium would burn right through the concrete base of the plant and into the earth. Another term for meltdown is the 'China Syndrome': an image (rather improbable) of the core melting all the way through to China! What's more likely is that the intense heat from the molten uranium would react with water in the containment vessel and/or with underground water, causing a steam explosion that would blow the containment vessel apart and spew radioactivity into the air.

A meltdown could release more radioactivity than a nuclear bomb. A deadly plume of radiation could be carried for miles with the wind. In the event of a meltdown, a government report prepared in 1964 predicts that about forty-five thousand people would be killed outright; one hundred thousand would be injured; and contamination would occur to "an area the size of Pennsylvania." This report was withheld from the public for eight years.[1]

Three Mile Island

How did the plant get made?
How did the plant leak?
What happens to people from radiation?
Why did they move pregnant women and young children, and not others?
How far would radiation spread if if blows up?
Would we have to go to another planet?
Why do they hide power plants behind trees and bushes?

Questions posed by K-2 class at Friends School, Cambridge, Mass.
New York Times,
April 6, 1979

The accident at Three Mile Island was set in motion on March 28, 1979 by a series of equipment failures, human errors, and design defects. The vital cooling water of the hot reactor was cut off by a faulty valve. The emergency backup water system went on automatically, but it too failed to function because two critical valves had been turned off two days before, following a routine maintenance check. The design of the reactor was so deficient, however, that there was no gauge, no lights, no buzzers—anything—to warn the control room operators that, although the emergency system was on, no cooling water was circulating because of the closed valves! And finally, the plant's pressurizer-level indicators, which monitor the pressure and temperature in the reactor cooling system, malfunctioned, leading the operators to believe the water level was adequate. They therefore proceeded to turn off the safety systems!

As a result, the reactor core was uncooled for as long as eleven hours and temperatures rose to thirty-six hundred degrees! It is clear that the top of the core was uncovered and a partial meltdown occurred. A further danger was that the cooling water reacted with the overheated fuel rods to produce an unanticipated hydrogen gas bubble. This bubble prevented the complete cooling of the fuel rods and threatened its complete meltdown. For four days, the scientists were baffled by this freak situation until the mysterious bubble reduced in size of its own accord. A catastrophic event was averted . . . this time.

I see the spectacular series of failures happening one after the other as a slap at the arrogant nuclear proponents who claim the perfection of their technological baby.

Nancy

It's pretty incredible, and so appropriate, that one of the control room operators during the accident was called Faust!

Henna

The nuclear industry never said this thing in Pennsylvania would never happen. With the amount of time reactors have been operating, it was time for it to happen. It shows our predictions were pretty good—that should be reassuring to the public.

James Dodson
Ohio Edison nuclear spokesman[2]

My eight-year-old daughter had heard about the accident on TV and wanted to know what a meltdown was. I was in a terrible panic but took the time to talk to her. My husband joined me and we tried to explain, as best we could, what a meltdown was. I could sense that Alyssa really needed to know what was going on. Her reaction was really beautiful. She saw it as a crisis, but she reacted with strength and she said she knew it would be okay. I could see that she was trying to calm me down. There is so much hope in children. It is so important that we build on that hope and justify it. It was a difficult time, but just sharing the information and the feelings really brought unity to our family.

Carolyn

What does radioactivity mean?

Many naturally occurring elements are unstable or *radioactive*. They are radioactive because unstable atoms cannot exist forever in nature and tend to become stable by giving off streams of particles and energy waves from the nucleus inside each atom. The stream of waves and particles is known as *radiation*. This emission process, giving off radiation, is known as *radioactive decay*. The decay takes place until the element becomes stable. The process can take fractions of a second or thousands of years, depending on what the element is.

In a nuclear reactor, radiation is produced when the uranium atom is split in the fission process. The resulting fission fragments are generally unstable and emit radiation.

What are the different kinds of radiation?

There are three types of radiation given off by radioactive elements: alpha and beta particles and gamma rays. Each type affects our bodies in different ways. Some types stay in the body and irradiate body cells for a long time, and others go through the body at great speed, damaging cells on the way.

Alpha particles are large and carry a lot of energy. They don't penetrate very far, but because they give off a lot of energy, they can do serious harm to our body cells.

Beta Particles are eight thousand times smaller in terms of mass than alpha particles, and consequently faster, so they can penetrate very far in matter. They can travel through a number of body cells before they lose energy and come to a stop. Both alpha and beta particles do most damage to body cells if they are ingested with food and water or inhaled with the air we breathe.

The third kind of radiation is *gamma radiation*. Gamma rays are similar to X-rays. They have the greatest penetrating power, and can go right through our bodies.

How does radiation harm us?

All matter, including our body cells, is made up of atoms. An atom has a nucleus with a positive charge and is surrounded by electrons of an equal negative charge. When radiation passes through an atom it can expel one or more electrons. When an atom loses an electron, it becomes unbalanced with the extra positive charge. It is now a charged *ion*. Too many in a cell can cause chemical changes that are destructive. Because of this process, radiation that harms us is known as *ionizing radiation*. Alpha and beta particles, X-rays, and gamma rays are all types of *ionizing radiation*.

All cells of the body have a central nucleus which contains genes, the basic inherited material which controls all our characteristics (eye color, hair, facial characteristics, enzyme systems, etc.). Genes are changed by radioactive particles into mutated genes. . . . If a gene in the sperm or egg cell is altered by radioactive particles, the new baby will be born either with an inherited disease or the baby may appear normal but will transmit the damaged gene to future generations to become manifest in later years.[3]

Is there a safe level of radiation?

Doses of radiation are measured in units called millirems and millirads. The Environmental Protection Agency (EPA) has arbitrarily set a maximum permissible level of radiation at five hundred millirems per person per year. The safety of the standards has been seriously in question for the past decade, and many studies are showing that levels far below the "permissible" are dangerous. The International Commission on Radiological Protection and the National Council on Radiation Protection have agreed to base their dose-response estimates on the assumption that *there is no safe level of radiation.*

In 1970 the Atomic Energy Commission (AEC, now the Nuclear Regulatory Commission and the Department of Energy) instructed two doctors, John Gofman and Arthur Tamplin, to study the effects of low-level radiation. But when they found that the risks of cancer, leukemia and genetic damage were far greater than they had believed, the AEC refused to publish their results. Newer studies by Dr. Thomas F. Mancuso and Dr. Alice Stewart have substantiated and further extended their findings. The EPA standards however, remain unchanged.

If low-level radiation is a problem for the general population, it is even more of an immediate problem for those working at nuclear power plants. There is a discrepancy between the exposure level of the ordinary person and that of the worker. According to EPA standards, workers can be exposed to five thousand millirems per year. The reason for the difference is that the standard-setters assumed that the nuclear industry could not afford to expose their workers to less radiation and still maintain a profitable industry. In this case, as in so many others, profit takes precedence over the health of the workers.[5]

Cancer is a danger to the individual; genetic defects are a threat to the human race.[4]

During the accident at TMI, there were accidental as well as planned releases of large quantities of radioactive gases. The planned releases, initially denied by Metropolitan Edison who owns the plant, were meant to reduce the dangerous pressure level within the containment vessel of the nuclear reactor. The gases released contained radioactive xenon and krypton. On March 29, the day after the accident, four hundred thousand gallons of radioactive water were dumped into the Susquehanna River without any warning to towns and cities downstream. Inert gases such as xenon and krypton were also released into the air, but the Nuclear Regulatory Commission (NRC) did not monitor radiation levels at the beginning of the accident when the largest amounts escaped. Planned radiation emissions continued for months after the accident.

One of a series of misleading statements by the NRC was that the radiation received by residents near TMI was not very much, only as much as "a dental X-ray." But the "X-rays" went on for hours and days! And dental X-rays affect only a small portion of the jaw; at TMI, people's entire bodies were exposed to radiation. The threat to public and environmental health is by no means over at TMI; the plant's containment vessel is still full of radioactive substances.

Something's wrong with the air. My mommy told me it could kill me.
> Six-year-old, Hershey, Pennsylvania,
> *New York Times*, April 16, 1979

Our teacher said on Friday that when the plant got built, the government promised there'd be no radiation. It wouldn't leak out on us. What are they going to say the next time this happens?
> Child in Middletown, Pennsylvania,
> *Boston Globe*, April 1980

Shut them down before it's too late. Amen. Shut them down before it's too late, any way you can, but shut them down. Get those plants shut down because if you don't, you're going to be paying the price just like we're paying here. You're never going to have any peace of mind as long as those plants are running. Shut them down. Shut them down. Any way you can, but shut them down.[6]

For whom is radiation most unsafe?

Because the body cells of fetuses, babies, and children are rapidly dividing and growing, they are most susceptible to radiation. Also, the National Academy of Science states that the risk of developing cancer due to radiation exposure appears to be "twice as great for women as men."[7]

How can radiation get into the body?

Gamma radiation, like X-rays, can penetrate the body from outside. Radioactive particles such as alpha and beta particles do not penetrate far but, if breathed in with the air, can damage our cells.

Radioactive particles can also enter the food chain and through the food chain enter our bodies. For example, strontium 90, a radioactive fission product, can settle on grass; it can then be eaten by cows and concentrated in their milk. Children, who are heavy milk drinkers, receive a large dose of strontium 90. If a mother ingests strontium 90, it can concentrate in her breast milk, which is then passed on to her baby. Strontium 90 is chemically similar to calcium, so in the body it is received like calcium and absorbed into the bones where it can cause bone cancer.

If radioactive particles get into water, they can then be taken in by fish and passed to humans who eat the fish. Iodine 131 can enter the body through cow's milk as well as through fish. Iodine 131 is concentrated by the human thyroid gland and is particularly dangerous to young children.

An important thing to remember about radioactive particles is that they concentrate further at each step of the food chain. Also, radioactive particles can accumulate in the body with each additional exposure. Absorbed into the body, they decay radioactively for years, damaging cells continuously. Radioactive particles are therefore different from X-rays or gamma rays, which pass through the body but do not accumulate there.

I worried about fresh produce. It was difficult for me as a mother to ignore my fears that I might be slowly poisoning my children each time I fed them.
Mother in Pennsylvania
Redbook, April 1980

At TMI, only the external gamma rays were monitored by the NRC. They never monitored radioactive particles in the air.

When I think about the power plants, I think they're not good because if they let off too much gas or energy, Pennsylvania or Somerville or Boston could be like a deserted area. Lots of people could be destroyed. if too much radiation gets into everybody's body, including cats and dogs and even plants, they could die in seconds or minutes or even years. I want especially children to know this. The parents who are reading this should tell their children that the radiation hurts kids more than grown-ups. All the people out there that are reading this story will want to know how the radioactivity gets into their bodies. I'm telling you now and I'm warning you. It could go in lakes and get into fish. It could come out of our drainpipes. When we're taking a shower and we shampoo our hair, we could get some in those little holes in our skin. We can even breathe it into our noses and it could ruin our lungs. So help to stop nuclear energy. It's the only way we can survive.

Ned, seven years old

Radiation makes you get sick, really sick. The cells go coo-coo.
Taras, seven years old
Cambridge, Massachusetts

What's so awesome about radiation is that you can't see it or smell it but it is there. You can only experience it by its effects.
Lynn

How long does radiation stay around?

As stated earlier, radioactive particles decay, or give off radiation, until they become stable. The time it takes for a radioactive particle to become stable is different for each element and is measured in half-lives. A half-life is the length of time it takes for a radioactive substance to lose half of its radioactivity. For example, zirconium 95 has a half-life of sixty-five days. This means that half of the zirconium will lose its radioactivity in sixty-five days, half of the remaining half in the next sixty-five days, and so on.

Iodine-131 has a short half-life of eight days. Strontium 90 and cesium 137 have half-lives of about thirty years. Plutonium 239 has an amazingly long half-life of twenty-five thousand years. It is dangerous, therefore, for at least 250,000 years. Moreover, it is a particularly harmful element; even if one dust particle of plutonium is inhaled, there is grave danger of getting lung cancer.

In November, 1981, potassium iodide pills were distributed to 7000 families who live near the Sequoyah nuclear plant because they may not have enough time to flee in case of a nuclear accident. A spokeswoman for the Tennessee Health Department said state officials came up with the plan "because evacuation routes may become clogged and people fleeing radiation could become contaminated before they get far enough away."[8]

During the accident at Three Mile Island, the surrounding population, young and old, was not protected. It is clear that the government and the nuclear industry were completely unprepared for a major nuclear accident. Plant officials did not understand what was happening inside the plant as the problem developed. Human and mechanical errors compounded each other. No one—city, state or federal officials, plant officials, or the media—could be trusted to give us accurate information about what was happening. In retrospect, it seems as though the primary consideration of the plant and federal officials was to preserve the image of nuclear power, not the safety of people.

There was no established chain of communication from plant to public, and no feasible evacuation plan. Pregnant women and children were exposed to fifty-six hours of radiation, until finally, on March 30, Governor Thornburgh suggested that it might be "wise" for pregnant women and preschool children to evacuate if they lived within five miles of the plant. At a noon press conference, Governor Thornburgh conceded that the unborn and the very young are most susceptible to fallout. The directive's outrageous implication was that others, kindergarten children for instance, or pregnant women living six miles from the plant, were out of danger!

At least 200,000 people saw through the propaganda and fled the area. At one point, Harrisburg residents mistakenly thought a broken siren was an evacuation alert. Panic followed, and within fifteen minutes, traffic in that city was hopelessly snarled. In the event of a complete meltdown, it would have been absolutely impossible to evacuate the 950,000 people of the surrounding areas.

U.S. Surgeon General Julius Richmond sent massive quantities of potassium iodide tablets to Harrisburg residents to minimize the effects of radioactive iodine, but they were never distributed because Governor Thornburgh and Metropolitan Edison did not want to cause public panic.[9]

Last Friday, when the school principal told everybody to go home, Langston ran across the street to his house and turned on the television so there would be some sound in the house to comfort him. He was alone; both parents work. While Langston tried to watch a cartoon, he began to cry. He thought he was going to die without his mother and father. He called the factory where his mother works. "Is this an emergency call?" the operator at the factory asked him. "Yes," Langston told her. "Leave a message and we'll have her call you back," the operator said. "I want her now," Langston said. Langston held on while the operator had someone go out on the plant floor to get his mother. When his mother heard her son crying over the phone, she left work, went home and packed a bag and took him to relatives in Rome, New York. Langston came back to Middletown because the television set said the schools in town were open. They were not. "Everyone just lies," he was saying. They all lied. They'll lie next time too."[10]

When will the effects of radiation show up?

With high levels of exposure, the lethal effects are obvious immediately. The problem with lower levels is that there is a time-lag between initial exposure to radiation and its effects. Subsequent leukemia or cancers may appear five to twenty years later. For this reason, it is difficult to prove that radiation is the cause of the illness.

Genetic effects may not appear for a few generations. If a gene in the sperm or egg is damaged by a radioactive particle, the baby may be spontaneously aborted or born with a birth defect or inherited disease. Or the baby may appear normal but pass on a defective gene to later generations. In the future, if two people with defective genes mate, the baby will show the effects of radiation. There are about two thousand diseases caused by genetic mutations, among them cystic fibrosis and dwarfism.

What will this mean for us in the long run?

Dr. Rosalie Bertell is a mathematician and medical researcher. In *Nuclear Witnesses, Insiders Speak Out*, Dr. Bertell tells of her concerns about the dangers of the increasing radiological burden we all share.

The problem is escalating dangerously. 'Increasing radiation in our environment is producing more of these mild mutations, people who are already genetically damaged when they're born and less physically able to cope with a radiation environment. Now you can't continue to increase the number of people in a population with mild mutations at the same time as you increase radiation pollution that they are not able to handle. As far as I'm concerned, this is a death process in the human species.'

Bertell fears that by the time people realize what is happening, there will be so much radiation in the environment that it will be too late. In addition to the normal radioactive emissions from nuclear plant operations, the 'military is setting off two to three bombs a week in Nevada, blasting an incredible amount of radioactivity into the desert floor and venting some radioactive gases into the atmosphere.' People are unaware of the increasing danger to their health. 'They don't even know what to look for, if exposed. All they know is that they might die of cancer, but what they're experiencing is acceleration of the aging process. They have no idea that when they get heart disease, that it's at a younger age than they would've gotten it had they not been exposed to radiation.'

Furthermore, people have no idea of the effect of radiation on children. 'Take, for example, a nuclear worker who has a child with dysentery. He doesn't know that that sickness may be connected to his work. He just thinks it's something unfortunate. People don't realize that the effects of radiation in children can be increases in asthmas, allergies, rheumatic fever, pneumonia, dysentery, besides the leukemias and cancer and any chronic diseases with a genetic component.'

With what she has seen and what she knows, Bertell cannot be silent. 'We are in a crisis,' she says, 'a big crisis.'[11]

What is the accident record in nuclear power plants?

The accident at TMI helped many of us to realize that there has been a sleeping giant in our midst for a long time and we have been negligently unaware of its existence. The TMI accident was not the first warning; there have been other serious accidents.

"Minor" spills and leaks occur frequently. Some plants steadily leak small amounts of radioactivity, and others have had ruptured pipes and explosions, temporarily releasing large amounts of radiation for short periods. Still others have accidentally spilled thousands of gallons of radioactive water into nearby waterways. In 1976, the Vermont Yankee plant spilled eighty-three thousand gallons of liquid waste, containing tritium, into the Connecticut River. Some nuclear plants, such as Diablo Canyon in California and Indian Point in New York, are built very close to major earthquake faults.

In 1975, a workman started a fire with a candle at the Brown's Ferry plant in Alabama. This nearly led to a meltdown. Since TMI, there has been a serious accident at the Robert I. Ginna plant in Ontario, New York. In January 1982, failure of a critical valve produced a steam bubble that could have led to overheating and damage of the core. In a study of 19,400 "events" at nuclear power plants from 1969 to 1979, Critical Mass Energy Project found 169 incidents that could have lead to core meltdowns.[12]

The newspapers are no longer writing much about TMI, but that doesn't mean the accident is over. The effects will continue in the leukemias and cancers that will appear years from now. It may be difficult to prove the connections to radiation exposure, but already it is clear that something is very wrong in the area surrounding the plant.

Farmers and veterinarians report abnormally high genetic defects in animals, as well as an astonishing increase in miscarriages and Caesarian sections. Plants are growing deformed and dwarfed and blooming unseasonally.

Among human children, the genetic effects will take longer to show up. But already Pennsylvania health officials have confirmed a fourfold increase in hypothyroidism, or low thyroid function in newborn babies. This condition can be caused by exposure to iodine 131.[13]

There have been reports of higher than normal rates of miscarriages and stillbirths as well as of divorces and suicides. There is no measure for the stress and psychological trauma created by those terror-filled days which live on in the parents' fearful concerns for their children.

Sooner or later, something genetic is going to show up in one of those children. The big thing is trying to prove it. It's only when you see a very high increase of cancer and genetic effects in the children who were left standing, waiting for a bus, waiting to get into a school building. And all the while this stuff was pouring out of that plant. It is so incredible that I can't imagine in my wildest dreams why those people weren't arrested on the spot and charged with criminal negligence, because that's what it was. Those children are going to grow up and we don't know what we might be confronted with.[14]

Jane Lee,
A farmer living near TMI

I don't want to die young.
Child in Middletown,
Pennsylvania, after the accident
at Three Mile Island
Boston Globe, April 6, 1979

Is the danger from radiation limited to the nuclear plant itself?

No. The entire process, known as the nuclear fuel cycle, is hazardous to health and life. At the head and tail of this monster lurk many dangers.

The fuel cycle begins with the *mining* of uranium. In the United States, the largest uranium deposits are located in the Southwest. The miners, most of whom are Native Americans, are exposed to radon gas during the mining process. It is estimated that up to twenty percent of the uranium miners die of lung cancer.

After it is brought up from the earth, the uranium must be refined through *milling*, which produces thousands of tons of radioactive pieces, called tailings. Until recently, these tailings were carelessly left lying around in heaps. Some people used the tailings to build homes and schools, only to find later that they were highly radioactive.

The next step occurs when uranium is *enriched* and fabricated into fuel rods. The workers involved in this process are at risk. The *transportation* of the uranium fuel rods on our highways poses the serious threat of contamination to both rural and city populations.

During the fission process in the reactor, enormous quantities of radioactive fission fragments are produced, creating a dangerous radioactive *waste* problem. Finally, at the end of the fuel cycle is the tail of the monster, the nuclear plant itself. After thirty or forty years, it becomes too radioactive for further use. This huge, radioactive container must be dismantled, or *decommissioned*. The costs involved in taking apart a radioactive power plant are astronomical. Another idea is to encase the whole beast in concrete, in which case it will stay with us as a monument to our times.

Egypt had its pyramids; India, the Taj Mahal. The mark of the twentieth century will be its radioactive nuclear power plants.
Helen

Why do we have nuclear power?

By the end of the last World War, hundreds of thousands of workers had been part of the production of the atomic bomb, and billions of dollars had been invested. Powerful economic and political interests had no intention of allowing the atomic industry to disappear. Government and military leaders developed a plan to encourage public acceptance of a continuing atomic weapons program. As a part of this plan, they decided to promote the "peaceful" use of atoms in the form of nuclear energy. Nuclear power was sold to the public with the claim that it was safe, clean, and incredibly inexpensive. This served to transform the atom's image from deadly to respectable.

Nuclear plants are not safe, but are they a cheap source of energy?

The expenses involved in building a nuclear power plant are the largest single factor in determining the price of nuclear electricity. These costs have been rising at three times the rate of inflation. The costs of operating a nuclear plant are rising as well. By the late 1980 s, nuclear electricity may be nearly double the costs of electricity generated by coal power.[15]

The price of uranium increased forty-five percent over the past year. What we don't hear about are the hidden costs of nuclear power: the cost of decommissioning or dismantling the power plant after thirty years, the cost of storing waste for a half a million years, the cost of research and development, not to mention health costs that individuals and society must bear.

The low cost estimates from the nuclear power industry are overly optimistic and based on generating capacity figures that a nuclear plant never actually achieves. If there is a shutdown at a nuclear power plant, the industry has to buy energy from fossil-fuel generating plants. Nuclear plants shut down frequently, as a result of accidents and for maintenance reasons, and the costs for this go straight into our bills via the "fuel adjustment clause." So we are paying for the costs of shutdowns as well as for the high construction and operating costs of the plants themselves.

Metropolitan Edison announced after the accident (at Three Mile Island) that it would go bankrupt unless the customers shouldered much of the financial burden of the accident.[16]

How does the problem of nuclear waste threaten all children and the very future of life on earth?

In all industries, at the end of the cycle there are waste products to be dealt with. In the case of nuclear plants, the waste poses more than ordinary problems because it is radioactive for hundreds of thousands of years. The government estimates that by the end of this century there will be more than eleven million cubic feet of low and high level nuclear waste in the United States alone.[17]

When radioactive wastes enter the environment, they contaminate land and water and can cause cancer and leukemia in human beings and animals. Making sure that radioactive waste products do not come in contact with living things for vast stretches of time is proving to be an enormous problem. Radioactive wastes are now located in temporary sites, which are rapidly filling up. Leaks and spills have begun to occur, and there is great pressure to come up with a solution.

During the Carter administration, the government took over responsibility for disposing of radioactive wastes, allowing the utilities to get off the hook by paying a one-time fee. Essentially, the burden has fallen on the shoulders of the taxpayers to pay for all disposal.

As yet, there is no permanent solution. Concern is rising that quick, politically expedient solutions are dangerous in the long run. Disposal suggestions include salt-mine and ocean-bed burial. Early experiments with salt mines in Lyons, Kansas, proved disastrous because leaching water made the mine unsafe for radioactive wastes. The ocean-bed proponents suggest that radioactive waste be buried in underwater valleys and plains on the sea floor. But there is no guarantee that an earthquake, or the natural movement of the mysterious sea, would not trigger a massive, contaminating accident. Decisions made today will affect all of us, and all future generations.

I can't understand why this industry was allowed to begin without having a solution to one of its major problems. I guess it's the arrogance of technology to believe that for every problem there is bound to be a technological solution.

Hayat

Mom, if it's so bad, why is there nuclear power?

Taras
seven years old

In the meantime, the temporary storage pools for spent fuel rods located near power plants are filled to capacity. In the face of this, the utilities are seeking permission to fill them up even more by reducing the amount of space between the fuel rods. This compaction will dangerously increase chances of starting a chain reaction.

As the public becomes more aware of the problem of nuclear waste, governors and residents of different states have become reluctant to allow waste-disposal sites in their own backyards. So far, up to seven states have moratoriums banning the construction of nuclear plants until a solution has been found to the nuclear waste problem. Because this problem is an inherent part of the nuclear power economy, it is becoming a focal point for organizing against nuclear power.

Soon after the accident, a commission was set up to study the causes of the accident. The Kemeny Commission, as it was named after its chairman, was a mixed blessing. Although it exposed gross negligence on the part of the Nuclear Regulatory Commission (the government watchdog overseeing nuclear operations) it did not come out with any strong recommendations such as a moratorium on nuclear power.

Among the problems exposed by the commission, the principal one is that essentially, the NRC allows the nuclear industry to regulate itself. The Inspection and Enforcement division of the NRC rarely enforces rules against safety violations, even repeated ones. The NRC ignored information that pointed to serious problems in the type of reactor that was produced by the Babcock and Wilcox Company for Three Mile Island, as well as many other nuclear power plants across the nation. Negligence on the part of the NRC and the industry brought us to the brink of a catastrophe.[18]

In spite of these findings, the commission did not choose to make any definitive recommendations, but instead said the final decision about nuclear power should be made through the political process. In our experience, this process has effectively left out the opinions of the concerned public.

A scrutiny of the federal energy budget over the years continues to confirm a bias in favor of nuclear energy. The 1984 budget proposes 816 million dollars for nuclear energy spending compared to only 253 million dollars for solar and all other renewable energy sources.[19]

In spite of the government push for nuclear power, the nuclear industry is in trouble. We are finding the nuclear industry slowing down of its own accord because of economic pressures. Over the last five years, at least seventy nuclear units have been cancelled and the outlook for future nuclear power projects is so dim that General Electric, once a leading reactor manufacturer, has said it doesn't expect any orders for nuclear plants this decade.[20] Two reasons for this are decreased public demand for extra electricity and escalating construction costs. All across the nation, nuclear projects are collapsing because of huge cost overruns.

What has happened since the Three Mile Island accident?

We should be increasingly vigilant about the nuclear waste situation. The public needs to have a say on where and how nuclear waste will be dumped. We need to make sure that speedy and unsafe means of waste disposal do not become accepted.

Another crucial debate is whether consumers should be required to shoulder most of the costs for abandoned nuclear projects. Unless we fight against it, the consumers and taxpayers will end up subsidizing the most troubled projects, including the cleanup costs of Three Mile Island. What we have to look forward to is continual rate hikes. Our cheap energy source has turned into the proverbial albatross.

The final issue for us to face is our own failing memories. In each of our lives, there are so many urgent, daily concerns it takes an act of will to make a leap into a larger struggle. We may not always have the time or the energy. It is also depressing to think of radiation and meltdowns and we have all found ourselves, at different times, simply

What are the key nuclear issues to keep in mind today?

not wanting to think about it. In this media-haunted life of ours, big, splashy coverage of a nuclear accident can rouse our consciousnesses. When the accident occurred at Three Mile Island, public consciousness soared. Many more anti-nuclear groups (including our own) were formed that year than ever before or after. But with time the feeling of danger has passed and it is difficult to sustain a sense of urgency and confrontation with the nuclear industry. But absence of coverage by the media does not mean that the problem has disappeared. There are daily spills and contamination, and the nuclear waste problems continue to be a nightmare. A Ralph Nader organization report said that more than four thousand nuclear reactor mishaps occurred in 1981, 140 of them of major significance. The report continued that it is just a "matter of time" before another serious accident occurs.[21] Even the nuclear industry has changed its tactics. Industry spokespeople no longer claim that there are no dangers inherent in a nuclear-based economy, but rather pass them off as being a "necessary risk."

In these times, having a child is an act of hope. But with that hope comes a responsibility to do everything in our power to ensure that our children have a chance to grow up healthy and happy in a world free of radiation, pollution, and war. From our children's own hopes and visions, we can draw inspiration and strength for our struggle.

Dear presedent Carter.
I'm Worried abute nucks.
Some Day Someone you know
Will be hurt or killd by
nucks and than you
Will thingK I wish I had
stopt nucks whene I Was
presedent But than it will
be to late. US Chidran need
a safe World to grow up in.
Whene the grown ups where
Chidrain
your mothers took
care of you. and now it's
your turn to take care
of us and if you don't
you won't have any
gradchidrin and not a

safe World.
           Sincerely
              maya

Nuclear Weapons

In this chapter, we discuss the history of the nuclear arms race, the use of nuclear weapons in World War II, and the possiblities of their use again in some future conflict. As in the Nuclear Power section of the book, we touch briefly on many aspects of the problem: the dimensions of possible destruction, the short and long term impact of the use of such weapons, the cost and politics behind specific weapons systems, and our own and our children's responses to the fact of possible nuclear holocaust.

Again, we make no pretense of covering all of the aspects of the nuclear weapons problem. We hope to give parents a handle on the situation and the political and economic underpinnings involved.

We realize that with this topic, information is not necessarily liberating. In fact, the more we researched nuclear weapons, the more scared we became. Still, knowing what the politicians were talking about, having some understanding of the state of research and development of weapons systems and being able to connect this information with information about nuclear power helped us to see the realities that we face in a larger and more comprehensive way. For parents who would like to learn more, there are some good starting places listed in the Resource Section.

No matter what country started a nuclear war, our whole world could go out like a light bulb and there would be no one to turn it on.

Once, when asked about the possibility of World War III, Einstein said, " I don't know when it will start. But I know for sure there will be no World War IV." He was very concerned that the power of mass destruction would be concentrated in the wrong hands, and devoted the last part of his life to peace work. Einstein was convinced that all citizens need to understand atomic energy, and participate in decision-making about the uses of the new technology.

It was Einstein's theories that had shown scientists the way to unleash the tremendous power of the atom. In 1905 he came up with his famous formula, $E = mc^2$. (The "E" stands for energy, "m" for mass, and "c" for the speed of light.) The theory expressed by this formula was scientifically revolutionary, because it suggested that a very small amount of matter could be turned into a tremendous amount of energy. Scientists in many parts of the world began to study the idea and experiment with it. Over a period of years, it became clear that with the right materials and the right process, it would be possible to force the nucleus of an atom to give up its energy in an enormous explosion.

In 1938, scientists succeeded in splitting an atom of uranium. The first bomb to be built on the principle of nuclear fission was exploded in New Mexico on July 16, 1945, and on August 6, the Japanese city of Hiroshima was destroyed by an atomic explosion. A similar explosion leveled the city of Nagasaki three days later.

In 1945, there came into the world a new image—the image of exterminating ourselves with our own technology.

Robert J. Lifton

Never Again

The bombings of Hiroshima and Nagasaki marked the first time that radiation had been used as a method of destroying life. Many people were killed instantly, and many more died within a few weeks of the blast, from burns and radiation poisoning. In all, 250,000 children, women, and men lost their lives.

Survivors describe the aftermath of the attack as a living hell. Called *Hibakusha*, these survivors see themselves as having a special responsibility to promote peace. They have written poems and books, painted pictures, made films, and gone on countless speaking tours—to tell the people of the world what it was like, to insist it must never happen again. With growing alarm, they have watched the world prepare for another nuclear conflict.

Hiroshima survivor Tazu Shibama, speaking at an anti-nuclear rally in Boston in 1980 gave a large, silent crowd her firsthand account of

Rest in peace, for the mistake will not be repeated.
Memorial at Hiroshima

the devastation. Then, looking out at the horrified faces of her audience, the seventy-four-year-old teacher said quietly, "War is no good. War does not solve anything. Bombs, no matter how big they are, cannot give the answer. The only thing that can bring the answer is peace, happiness, and friendship."

They Call This Security?

Why didn't the world's deep shock at the destruction of Hiroshima and Nagasaki stop the nuclear weapons industry in its tracks? At the end of World War II, the United States government promised the people of the world that in the future, nuclear energy would be used only for peaceful purposes. American scientists began to think of ways to make electricity with nuclear power, telling us it would be a safe and inexpensive way to meet our energy needs. Quietly, shaded by the "peaceful" atom, government scientists continued to think of ways to make bombs with nuclear technology—bigger bombs with more destructive power.

In 1949, the Soviet Union exploded its first test nuclear weapon. The people of the United States were told that we needed *more* destructive power or the Russians would destroy us. The people of the Soviet Union were told that the United States would destroy them if they did not step up their own weapons development. The arms race was on.

The Hopi Prophecy

Native Americans are among those who have suffered most severely from the U.S. nuclear weapons program, since their lands and their lives have been laid waste by the mining of uranium.

Thomas Banyacya is a Hopi Indian and the last surviving "Messenger" from a 1948 council of that nation's spiritual leaders. For the past twenty-two years, Banyacya has been warning Indians and whites alike of a tragic fulfillment of an ancient Hopi prophecy: the end of the third phase of human life.

What was the message that you were to express to the world?

The message spoke of many things. There were many prophecies. One that I heard spoken of was that white man would make a thing made up of many things, the only word we have would mean "a gourd full of ashes," and it would be so powerful that if it dropped on the earth it would burn everything to ashes. It would be so hot that even things under water would die from the heat and nothing there would grow for many years. The prophecy was fulfilled with Nagasaki and Hiroshima.

But how will the world end?

We may burn ourselves up or we may have disturbed the balance of nature so much that there may be a great earthquake, or a great wind, or lightning or a great rain. All these forces of nature will start shaking us up. This is a warning to us now. We must keep the land according to the instructions we were given. The white man was given spiritual knowledge too, but he put that aside. [White Men] get greedy and they can't keep promises and they grab everything for themselves.[White Men] want so much. We don't know how to control it. There are uranium pits out there and their wastes are creating much cancer and disease. Now they are putting up bigger plants.

How have the Hopi tried to stop them?

[The Hopi] are trying in every way, but the government, with pressure from the big corporations, is pushing all the time to get in. They have the law and the money and the police and everything on their side. The Hopi are helpless. We are depending on the Great Spirit. We try to tell the white man, "Don't do it." because white man doesn't realize that they are getting to a really dangerous point. They are searching for more power and misusing that power. That is why we are so anxious to bring this message to the world.[2]

Testing Us All

During the years of above-ground testing of atomic weapons, thousands of servicemen were forced to witness nuclear explosions. Civilians in Utah and other Western states and on some Pacific islands were also exposed to radioactive fallout from atomic bomb tests. Many of these people are now dead or dying of cancer. Many more have given birth to children with severe birth defects and other serious health problems. Follow-up tests of the babies born to Marshall Islanders after their exposure to fallout in 1954 show that all the children eventually developed thyroid nodules or cancer.[3]

Although the government knew that exposure to radiation is associated with cancer and birth defects, this information was kept from the victims of nuclear testing. They were told their "participation" in the nuclear testing program had been a harmless exercise in patriotic responsibility. Thousands of these victims—sometimes called the "forgotten guinea pigs"—are suing the government for damages. But because radiation-related disease often takes many years to show up, the government maintains that it is impossible to "prove" a link between the tests and the health problems experienced later.

Since 1945 there have been more than one thousand test explosions of nuclear weapons worldwide, each one releasing deadly radiation into our environment. Above-ground testing in the United States and the Soviet Union was banned in 1962, but development and production of nuclear weapons continues unchecked. And just as in the nuclear power industry, radioactive wastes from weapons production are transported on our highways (sometimes through major population centers) and stored in inadequate temporary containment vessels.

Bombs being made today are one hundred times more powerful than the bombs dropped on Hiroshima and Nagasaki. The explosive power of nuclear weapons now in existence—ready to go—could destroy every living thing on this earth.

Every American (and Soviet) city with a population of over twenty-five thousand is targeted. It takes missiles about thirty minutes to get where they're going. In a full-scale nuclear war, it will all be over in about an hour.

Children know that this is not security. They know that this uneasy balance of terror threatens their lives and their world.

Consequences

Children and adults of the world:

At this very moment our future is being decided by adults who won't be alive to suffer the consequences of their nuclear inventions. People are deciding to build weapons, and they say that it's for their people. "Their people" should be able to decide if they want weapons or not. They have as many rights as presidents do to live and not suffer the after effects of a nuclear war.

I want to live and not suffer radiation and so do thousands of other children like me.

Nuclear weapons are dangerous and they should not be treated like toys. I am afraid for our futures. What would the world be like with no animals or people on it? What would the rivers and trees and mountains look like? Would the atmosphere be the same?

Kirsten Brown,
grade seven

If a twenty-megaton thermonuclear bomb were to hit the city of Boston, dead center, the downtown area would be instantly vaporized. People within ten miles of the blast would not survive the heat flash, the shock wave followed by three hundred MPH winds, and the fire storm (fueled by homes, oil tanks, natural gas lines, chemical storage containers, etc.).

Deadly radioactive fallout will blanket the area and begin to spread outward from the blast area. A study on how to minimize "excess radiogenic deaths" after a nuclear attack, commissioned by the U.S. Energy Department, recommends that elderly people be the first to leave shelters to search for uncontaminated food and water. The study suggests that old people, having lived most of their lives anyway, have "less to lose in terms of total life expectancy," so they should take the risk of going out into the poisonous air.[4]

But most civil defense officials have abandoned the fallout shelter plan, forced to admit that those in shelters will be asphyxiated. The government now says that mass evacuation of large cities may save some of us. In fact, the Federal Emergency Management Agency has plans to evacuate two-thirds of the U.S. population for "temporary relocation." But these civil defense plans, which cost millions of our tax dollars, are deceptive and misleading. While psychologically preparing the population for the next war, they also set up a false sense of security. Evacuation plans depend on at least a week's notice of nuclear hostilities. In reality, we'd probably have five to fifteen minutes notice of a nuclear missile attack. Anyone who's ever been caught in rush hour traffic knows how unworkable a mass evacuation would be. It's sometimes called "the last traffic jam."

An estimated 2.2 million children and adults will die right away. Millions of others will die later from radiation sickness, burns, and injuries. No one will come to help. Most of the hospitals and medical facilities will be destroyed. A growing number of doctors agree that the only medical treatment will be narcotics to numb the death agonies of the badly burned "survivors."

Food, water, and air will be contaminated. Communications will be cut off. Disposal of hundreds of thousands of corpses will be a major problem. It is often said that after a nuclear war, the living will envy the dead.

Once a nuclear conflict begins, it is very likely to escalate quickly. Thousands of highly accurate nuclear missiles are aimed at cities, at nuclear power reactors, at high-technology think tanks and chemical and biological warfare facilities. Most world leaders admit that if nuclear weapons are ever used, the result will be global destruction.

10/13/81

Dear President Reagan,

Why do you have to make nuclear weapons. I want to have a nice life without having to worry about getting killed in a war. They don't help anything but taking the risk of killing thousands of people. Don't you know what your doing. You want a lot of people getting killed if there is a war. Thats the way it looks right now. Please stop making nuclear weapons. I dont want to get killed when I'm about 15. I'm only 9. If you thought about it you might change your mind and care a little more. If you were me you might feel a little scared.   Jonathan Weinstock
age 9

Planning for the Unthinkable

One night my son runs into the kitchen and says, "Guess what I just heard on a news bulletin?"

"What?" I ask calmly. (My teeth are on edge. This was a week of extreme tension between Iran and the United States. A news bulletin could only mean trouble.)

He says, "Iran just sent up a satellite—with lasers! They're going to knock out all our satellites!"

(He's eight years old, and excited. Shades of Star Wars. But he's concerned, too—I can see it. His eyes search mine for reassurance.)

"They are? Well, let's watch the news together at eleven," I say evenly, in my mildly concerned tone. (The edges of my insides begin to curl. I start to sweat. What can it mean?)

Later, we watch the news, and it turns out he's got it all wrong. It hadn't been a news bulletin he'd seen, but the regular 10 P.M. update. What he had heard was some media speculation on the Soviet Union's rumored ability to use lasers over long distances. I though with relief, "Wow! For the last forty-five minutes I've been half-believing there's some kind of space war going on out there somewhere!"

A few days later, I glance at a newspaper lying on the kitchen table. A headline jumps out at me: "SOVIETS HAVE 'DEATH RAY,' U.S. BELIEVES." I think, did my little boy glance at that same headline this morning as he poured his breakfast cereal? My little boy, who understood the concept of laser disintegration from Star Trek reruns by the time he was four?

What a world. What are our children thinking?

Kate

Shopping List of Weapons Systems

The world is preparing for World War III. Over fifty countries now have all the materials and know-how they need to make nuclear weapons. There is a flourishing black market in nuclear weaponry; sabotage and theft of radioactive material occur frequently. Let's take a look at a few of the weapons systems our taxes are supporting.[5]

The Trident Sub. This is a nuclear-powered submarine, five stories high and over two football fields long. It's really a whole weapons system, very sophisticated and accurate. One of these subs carries enough explosive power to destroy three hundred cities. The cost of one Trident sub is $3.25 billion.

The Neutron Bomb. They call it a "radiation enhancement device." This warhead explodes with very little blast, but releases a large amount of radiation in the form of neutrons. The idea is to do as little damage as possible to buildings, tanks, and machinery, and as much damage as possible to living things. This bomb goes right for people; the neutrons attack the nervous system, causing immediate nausea, diarrhea, and convulsions. Depending on the dose, some people will die right away, others in a month or two. The rest of those exposed will be much more likely to develop leukemia and other cancers. Cost estimates for the production of the neutron bomb are over one billion dollars.

The MX (Missile Experimental). These missiles can travel eight thousand miles in half an hour, and hit within one hundred feet of the target. One MX missile carries more explosive power than all the bombs dropped during the Second World War, including Hiroshima and Nagasaki. Cost estimates for the whole system reach $100 billion!

These few examples illustrate the vast amounts of money and technical talent concentrated on mass destruction. There are already a few Tridents in operation, with more on the way. The neutron bomb and the MX are in the works. Soviet military leaders have equally frightening weapons on their shopping lists.

Yet both the United States and the Soviet Union can already destroy each other, and the rest of the world, many times over. These two countries now have the equivalent of four tons of TNT for every child, woman and man in the world.

Over five million people in the world are seriously malnourished; yet in pounds per person, the world has more explosive power than food. The gap between the world's rich and poor grows larger every year, yet governments spend four times more for research on weapons than on safe energy development.

Think of what society could do with all this money if we used it differently. One Trident sub costs more than the total amount of money the government spends in one year on mental health and alcohol and drug abuse education and prevention. Instead of spending one billion dollars on the neutron bomb, we could create eighty-five thousand jobs in mass transportation, 118,000 jobs in education. For a fraction of the cost of the MX missile system, we could lower property taxes; provide low-cost, quality day care for millions of children; begin a nationwide solar energy system; begin to clean up some of the hazardous chemical dumps that threaten the U.S. water supply. We can all think of better uses for our money.

But if leaders have so much sense, why have we had so many wars? And didn't they want that World War I to end all wars? Nobody even remembers why that one started, do they? [6]

Why is the world spending over one billion dollars a day on ways to destroy life? This question has been discussed in depth by some very creative thinkers, and we'll be referring to their writings in the resource section. In our view, it all boils down to profit and power. Huge economic and political interests are at stake.

Look at the U.S. and the U.S.S.R. Both nations have major economic, military, and political influence in countries outside their borders. Both the U.S. and the U.S.S.R. want to protect these spheres of power and expand them wherever possible. "Mutually assured destruction"(MAD), as the Pentagon strategists call it, is used as intimidation, to discourage interference. Smaller countries develop nuclear weapons in order to operate somewhat independently from the superpowers. The multinational corporations that dominate the world economy make huge profits from this competition for the biggest and baddest bang.

The relative prosperity the U.S. enjoys depends in part on the exploitation of the rich resources of Third World countries, like

"I hate war."

I hate war. Too many people get killed each year. . . .

I think that man because of his emotions will continue to kill each other and there is another kind of war besides killing people and that is killing our environment—the very essence of life we kill. People say we must kill for our ideas, but I can't think of one idea I would kill for because I don't think the idea is worth a damn if someone or something is killed. . . .

War is many things to many people. To some it is a game. To others a way to money. To me it's a waste of everything we've learned. . . .

Guatemala. In "The Peace Movement Today," Frank Brodhead talks about the reasons for the arms race:

I believe that the desire of the U.S. to maintain nuclear superiority over the Soviet Union stems from the role that nuclear weapons play in conventional conflicts or cases of U.S. intervention in the Third World. In a nutshell, the U.S. attempts to maintain nuclear superiority over the Soviet Union to prevent Soviet interference in U.S. military actions against nations striving for self-determination or; to break out of the U.S. economic sphere. Perhaps the best examples are the Korean and Vietnam Wars, in which the Soviet Union gave political and other support to forces opposing the U.S., but was careful to avoid any direct confrontation with the U.S.[7]

Of course, little of this makes sense to children. Kids' logic is connected to their deep and natural sense of rightness and wrongness. They know that love and health and the future are right; they know that planning for war is wrong.

Protest and Patriotism

Are we weakening the nation by protesting nuclear policies? Are we encouraging a Communist takeover by asking our leaders to negotiate world peace?

Some people think that criticism of the U.S. military-industrial establishment is 'giving comfort to the enemy', a traitorous act. They will ask questions like: "Why are you blaming the United States, and not the Soviet Union?" and "Would you want to live in Russia?" There are those who sincerely believe that if we love our country, we should support government policy no matter what. We should expect their questions.

Sometimes it helps to point out to our questioners that the Preamble to the U.S. Constitution claims for us the right and the responsibility to criticize and change what is wrong. We can also remind them that we are supporting U.S. (and not Soviet) military spending with our tax dollars. Residents of the U.S. are in a much better position to keep an eye on their own government than on the government of the U.S.S.R. It doesn't make sense for us to focus our social and political energy on the injustices of the Soviet Union. We have plenty of social and political problems to solve at home "in our own backyard."

How would you answer if your child asked:

Kate: The Soviet Union has a lot of nuclear weapons, just like the United States does. But I don't think we are "defending ourselves" with all those weapons. The nuclear build-up on both sides is doing just the opposite—making the world a more dangerous place.

Most Russians are ordinary people like us. They listen to music and go on picnics. The grown-ups work and the children play and go to school. And the Russian people are worried about all the nuclear weapons in the world too. The people of the world have to find ways to cooperate and get rid of all the nuclear weapons. It's a big problem, but I think that we can find the answer without violence, if we work together to find it. The U.S. and the U.S.S.R. need to find leaders who understand how to talk over problems and make peace.

Alice: At some point we have to dare to trust each other. Nuclear weapons are so terrible we are all afraid of them. We have to eliminate our own. We have always, with maybe one exception, led the way to developing weapons. We have to ask people to have a great deal of courage and faith that the Russians will also disarm. We don't need more weapons. They don't need more weapons. Maybe we're both terrified and everyone would feel very grateful if a stop was put to the arms race.

Hayat: With nuclear weapons we will simply destroy each other and perhaps the whole world. We can't think of nuclear weapons as "defense," since we will also be killed. The Russians understand this too. The only solution is for all nuclear countries to get rid of all their nuclear weapons. The problem is nobody wants to make the first move. At least the Russians have made some offers to dismantle their weapons if we will. We should take them up on that and negotiate to disarm together.

Ellie: Russia is a great big country like we are and they also have nuclear weapons. That's what makes it all so dangerous. They are scared of us and we are scared of them. Everytime we build a new weapon, they do too. Then we build more and they build more. That makes the world a very dangerous place.

The Russian people are people just like us. They are scared too. In Russia, people can't have demonstrations like we can here. But people over there are trying to let their leaders know that they don't want nuclear weapons. If we keep trying to get rid of ours, they will be encouraged to get rid of theirs. Nuclear weapons don't protect us. They make us more in danger.

72   *I think war is a bunch of men fighting over land, government, ownership and a lot of other things. People getting killed for something that can be talked out and maybe the problem [can be solved.] People being taken away from their family and friends that might not come back. Money being spent on war equipment that might just kill more men and women. Stuff like ships, guns, tanks, jets, and planes. Sure, war gets rid of some of the population, but in the wrong way.*[8]

Governments Are Not People

Maya: (aged eleven) "I don't know what the problem is between the Americans and the Russians. I like the Russians. They have beautiful music. I like Tchaikovsky and some great ballet dances come from Russia. Mummy, why do the Russians and Americans hate each other?

Hayat: (lamely) Well, it's not the people, the governments are the ones that don't like each other. Each government pretends the other is an enemy so they can build up their arms industry.

Maya: I think the people of Russia and the people of America should forget about the governments and get together and with our combined "smarts," we can get rid of all the nuclear bombs.

How would you answer if your child asked:

Kate: If it dropped right on us, or very close, we would die.

Alice: I would answer in a very matter-of-fact way that we would most probably die. But I would not detail how. Probably it would go on like this: I would stop for a bit and look at my child and say, "That would be so sad. Probably we would die." That might be the end of it. I would note that Hsuan loves Arlo Guthrie's song "The Un-neutron Bomb," which magically makes things disappear and leaves American and Russian soldiers, both male and female, suddenly running around without any clothes.

Hayat: It would give out a lot of radiation and a lot of people would get sick from it and die. The buildings we live in would get radiation in them, so we couldn't live in them for a long time. We would need to get ourselves to a safe place away from here. Many of us in the U.S., in Europe, and all over the world think this kind of bomb is cruel and unacceptable, and we are letting the government know how we feel about it.

Ellie: Lots of people would die right away from the blast. The people closest to where they dropped it would die. The people a little further away would die sometime afterwards from all the radiation. Lots more people would get very, very sick. Since we live in Cambridge, where lots of war plans and weapons plans are made, we would be right in the center of where the bombs would be dropped. We'd die right away—so quickly that we probably wouldn't even know it.

Barbara: We'd die.

"What would happen if a neutron bomb dropped on us?"

III. Alternatives

Changing Our Lifestyle

I feel as though I had my first ten years in the last scrap of time when you could count on water being clean, ground and food clear of pesticides and other toxins. Food was eaten in season and, as a result, we had countless celebrations as fruits and vegetables ripened. The earth was a whole and wonderful place; everything right and in scale.

During the postwar boom of the 1950s, all of this started to change. The oil economy created superhighways that tore through towns, leaving once-integrated communities staring across arbitrary chasms. Industrial pollution of air and water became commonplace. The convenience-food industry put food from everywhere on our table any time. The world no longer felt whole. Had we lost the earth, generations, seasons, place, rightness with our communities?

Alice

Land and wholeness figure prominently in American myth and legends. As Americans, we "love" this beautiful, abundant land, yet we soak it continuously with chemical and radioactive wastes. We strip-mine and build highways that destroy land and community. We allow the air and water to become poisoned, in turn poisoning ourselves and our children.

Children view life very concretely. They know what they need. But as a culture we have strayed a long way from such practical wisdom. What is it that has carried us away from this basic connectedness?

White Western tradition separates human beings from the physical world and our fellow creatures: plants, insects, stones, furry and feathered beings. In Western culture, we are set outside creation as special beings: namers of plants and animals. Fallen from paradise, we experience self-distrust, and keep ourselves apart from nature and each other. We are taught that the rest of the earth—minerals, water, soil, animals—are here for us to use as we wish.

White Europeans carried these ideas with them when they traveled to the "New World." America was *their* chance to start again, freed from the economic and religious oppression they had experienced in their homelands. They viewed the beautiful, fertile land as a New Eden that promised to nourish them both physically and spiritually. It was convenient for them to see it as a continent without history, a raw material to be developed at will, a gift from God. Many forgot, or did not recognize, that all of the earth's resources and creatures are finite, and that you must nourish life to sustain it.

Entire populations of Native America nations—children, women and men—murdered or removed from their lands. At the same time, millions of black Africans were kidnapped from their homes, sold into slavery (those who lived to reach America), and used to fuel the developing American system.

These exploitive attitudes also contributed to the form taken by the Industrial Revolution of the mid-nineteenth century. Businessmen and speculators benefited from the increased use of resources. Things could be made faster once machinery was part of production. There were thoughtful people at the time who cried out against the razing of the forests and the hastened exploitation brought about by this type of industry. Slave revolts, massive strikes, and resistance from Native Americans continued, but, then as now, money invested in money, and concentrated power.

America experienced a great boom following World War II. Traditional feelings of abundance and limitlessness, as well as privilege in the world, were expressed through new products, highways, airports. There was a feeling that we could go anywhere, have anything, in season or out, anytime we wanted. The generation born in the 1950s has grown up with this consumer society: buy it, use it, throw it out—there is plenty more to be had.

But the boom of the fifties and sixties drew heavily on our resources. Now, when we are beginning to realize that resources are limited, it is difficult to contemplate conservation. People don't want to be deprived of convenience.

How are we encouraged in the present day to continue on a course that is wasteful, that actually runs contrary to our needs and best interests, that continues to disconnect us from each other, the ground we stand on, our communities? Part of the answer lies in habit: we have become used to things being done in a certain way, to certain products being available, to certain ideas. We all set ourselves on a track, set our lives going, and forget to look around at the whole picture. Many of us have lost the ability to see how actions and decisions affect a community, a landscape, a water table, or people in another country.

One of the most dangerous disconnectors today is advertising—in magazines, on signs, and on television. Advertisements often use cherished messages and ideas to sell us products. Sometimes, it is very clear that we are buying ideas: a cigarette ad that proclaims the product to be "ALIVE WITH PLEASURE!" We know that smoking causes heart disease and cancer, but we love the advertisement picture of young people frolicking in the mountain greenery.

Other ads aren't so clear. The images pull us toward our roots, to a safer world of land and family. The emotional tug is toward decency and connection and love, while the product, by its very nature, furthers a process that takes us in exactly the opposite direction. The messages of such advertisements are subtly devastating because they work hard to devalue our own perceptions and judgments about ourselves and the world.

Here are some examples: In a TV ad for a supermarket chain, a cheerful grandpa in a cozy cardigan tells us that this is the "basic value store." He is shown on site at a family farm that supplies the supermarket. It is complete with beautiful red barn, happy people, and fields. However, most food produced for supermarkets is grown on huge acreages no longer owned by families. Managers run these farms, which rely heavily on oil-based fertilizers, herbicides and pesticides. Such farming practices are very expensive and result in a loss of tons of topsoil per acre per year. Without the precious layer of topsoil, nothing can be grown.

An ad for artificial lemonade, filmed in soft focus, exudes nostalgia for sweeter times past, when families gathered and lemons were real. In a country setting, once again, three generations are together on a hot summer day. A young woman brings out a frosty glass pitcher of lemonade and another grandpa says, "A-h-h, that tastes just like good old-fashioned lemonade, just like the kind I had when I was courtin' your grandma." Even though we know that real lemons still exist and that cross-generational gatherings occur, the message of the ad is powerful and disturbing: we have lost real food and real family, and are reduced to buying the idea of them with a box of lemon-flavored powder.

One illusion is much like another. A beautiful American landscape continues to be the backdrop, no matter the devastation we are being sold on. A glossy brochure advertising New England's nuclear power plants has two photographs on the cover: one of an old stone water mill, the other of Maine Yankee nuclear power plant. Above the pictures we see the words "Yankee Ingenuity." It is a reassuring phrase: just us folks taking care of ourselves, resourceful and independent. The brochure goes on to tell us that only large-scale, centralized power plants can produce significant and reliable amounts of electricity. Of course it tells us nothing about the truly ingenious Yankees who are installing solar collectors or starting up small-scale hydro-electric power plants again.

The military also uses everyday images to sell its products. Tools of potentially awful devastation are placed in the most casual of contexts. A McDonnell Douglas guided missile, with a nuclear warhead, pictured cruising along above the earth, simply "knows the lay of the land." Young men, lounging nonchalantly in crisp uniforms by the latest in rocket launchers (described as the "Simple System") might just as well be in clean jeans by their Chevy pick-up trucks, ready for a fun drive over unpaved country roads. At this level, the disconnection is complete. We have arrived at a terribly threatened position. How are we to reconnect ourselves with enough force to reverse the drift toward death?

> *One friend of mine once told me that she often had a feeling almost of remembering a time, as though it were just beyond memory, when we understood better our destiny, our place in the cosmos. More recently I heard a woman of the Wampanoag tribe say to a group of women, talking to us as representatives of our culture, "We don't understand you. We don't understand what your instructions are: how you have been taught to live. A seed, a flower unfolds according to the instructions it has been given. We don't understand yours." I guess we have forgotten.*
> Nancy Jack Todd[1]

As ponds turn brackish, as fish near nuclear power plants develop cancers, as we see children suffer terrible disease near waste dumps such as Love Canal, we are coming to appreciate that there are limits to what living organisms can tolerate. We are finally realizing something that people in other cultures have known all along; that the Earth is alive, after all, and as a living organism it has requirements for health as do human beings, plants, and all our fellow creatures. We are all here together.

Re-Grounding: Regaining Our Instructions

With a special urgency we are beginning to search out new connections, or perhaps to look at old connections in ways that will help us today. We feel as though our instructions are lost; many things in our culture confirm that they are. Yet they are there, if we choose to acknowledge them.

A navy ship fitted out with Raytheon detection and communications equipment speaks of danger, alertness on the seas, of a world ringed with destructive power. Nevertheless, the sea through which that navy ship glides is full of wonders, of life forms that haven't yet been discovered, ancient sea beds, many secrets.

If our instructions are those feelings, intuitions, ideas that connect us in living ways to each other and to the Earth, and if we have forgotten them, how can we reclaim this way of knowing? How can we learn to live with gratitude? Who can serve us as models, and how will we even know when we have found our right place to be?

Trusting our instincts: Rational analysis has become the most respected way of knowing, and yet intuitive understanding is often a clear, though neglected, way of perceiving what is happening. Thus, myths, fables, and fairy tales arising from this intuitive process continue to satisfy. "I've got a feeling . . ." may refer to a hunch or to sweaty palms, to contentment or sudden insight. By learning to know and trust our physical and emotional experiences we can often see through faulty analysis. Analysis has its place, but we must have courage and learn to trust our less conscious selves as well.

Our models might be provided by cultures, friends, people we have never met but who are important to us for their ideas or the example they set: artists, poets, Native Americans, grandparents, feminists—anyone or any group that has found a way of living which excludes the shortcut, the quick profit, the disconnected action that leads to wastefulness of life or land.

Looking deeply into our memories: we may be able to find long-forgotten songs or scents or stories that may help us.

"The other evening I reached out to pluck a sweet-smelling flower, and a long-forgotten voice whispered in my ears; "Don't touch, it's asleep!" Growing up in Bengal, we were taught that plants were much like us. They needed nourishment, had feelings, felt pain, and we were not to touch them at night, for they slept! As children we felt a precious kinship that I have gratefully recalled in a different culture, so many years later. In such simple, child's language, deep and long-lasting connections can be made.

Hayat

Being still: There are breathtaking miracles happening all around us. Beans grow, children grow, worms compost, the sun comes up. Our culture is too fast, too loud, pushes us too hard away from our centers, our roots. We have to find ways to still the noise around us, to calm the surface of the pond in order to see the reflection whole. Meditate, grow a garden, sit still and look, wherever you are, city or country. Still yourself and listen.

Sharing experiences: This is an ancient form of social interaction. We tell stories, we watch the reactions of others, and we learn from our telling and from the responses. Telling tales is a way of reflecting on our lives, and listening to them a way of discovering that we are all extremely different, yet ultimately the same. In a formal way, study groups can be a way of learning and sharing together. We can strengthen ourselves and each other by ending our isolation.

Breaking Out of the Box

Karen: Momma, can you turn off the TV? I want to go play, but I can't get away from the program.

Kate: Children are pressured to conform by TV, the schools, their peers, and by us—their parents. Only a small percentage of this conformity contributes to our survival or our happiness.

I make sure my son knows he is loved for his very self, so he feels safe in expressing himself in unusual ways if he chooses. We talk a lot about advertising and reality, people's beliefs and reality. He is learning that innovators and creative thinkers often have to walk a fine line in this assembly-line society. Those who wish to break old and useless taboos must usually establish a base for themselves of like-minded people, or risk being crushed by those who find their power or security in the status quo.

Hayat: Like many families, we are concerned about the influence of TV. I place limits on what they are allowed to watch and end up watching with them sometimes. When I do, I make critical comments on the programs as well as the commercials. I am sure I'm an irritating person to watch TV with, but I can't seem to stop myself when I watch the deception pouring out of the "box"! My children take me in good humor, fortunately, and the essential point seems to get through: that they don't have to accept unconditionally what they see and hear but can use their judgment to evaluate the messages. I would feel confidence about the future of the world if children simply listened to their own inner voices. They have so much good sense. I think the most important thing we can do for our children is to help them to trust themselves.

Barbara: By the time Toby and Karen were six, I faced the fact that even though they were alive and healthy, their childhoods were being eaten by TV. When I was busy I told them to go watch TV; when they were quarreling I told them to turn on the TV; when I was tired I watched TV and they would sit down with me.

The radiation that makes the TV picture is physically damaging to the human body. Although sets are shielded, I put the coffee table at the recommended two and a half feet from the tube and made a rule that no one could sit in front of it.

But watching TV is bad for them in other ways too. If they watched for more that an hour or so, they were wild and whiny afterward. I realized I had encouraged my kids to shut themselves up with images of people who are paid to pretend.

I asked other parents what they do, and the best advice I got was: "Put your foot down and grit your teeth until they adjust to being themselves instead of zombies."

Other helpful hints I sometimes use are:

—Tell them they have to do something else (without annoying you) for half an hour before they can watch TV. After a while my kids didn't want to stop what they were doing.

—Ask them to help you, or tell you a story, or just keep you company while you do your work.

—When you do watch TV, talk—like "That's a nice hairstyle," or "I think that's a dumb commercial," or "What do you think is going to happen next?"

Ellie: At our house, watching TV is a participatory experience. We talk back. In fact, we often yell back. Our daughter has grown up with the running dialogue and she's used to it. In fact, she joins in. Just now, I heard her telling the television in a sharp little voice: "That's not true. Women can be lawyers if they want to."

Changing Our Technology

Changing Energy

If nuclear power plants pose a risk to health in casual, everyday ways such as contamination of water, air, and shellfish beds as well as threatening destruction of life through accidental meltdown, then the risk is too high.

Energy, lifestyle, money, and health are intimately connected. Large, centralized power plants such as nuclear reactors cost a great deal of money to build, operate, and maintain. They must therefore be financed by those who have a great deal of money: banks and corporations. The investors will naturally choose to protect their investments at the expense of the consumer, whether that expense is measured in terms of dollars or health. Responsiveness to consumer concern would be too costly. But smaller, decentralized energy systems that can be owned by individuals or communities have a better chance of truly serving the needs of the people. The technology involved in small energy systems is more accessible because it is simpler and less expensive, making community decisions more practicable. Any technology can be misused, but the power systems that we think of as alternative energy—solar, wind generators, small hydro-electric generators—are much less likely to cause widespread injury to people or land because of their modest size and because they are nonpolluting.

The United States, like all of the Western world, runs on an energy-intensive economy. Ever-increasing amounts of fossil fuels—coal, oil, gas—are necessary to keep it all going.

Fossil fuels, currently our chief energy source, have played a key role in most of the economic and technological developments of the past hundred years, but most particularly in the years since 1950 when oil cost less than two dollars a barrel on the international market. Our way of life and our communities have been shaped by the use of cheap oil: throwaway products, our millions of cars and their companion highways that have changed the nature of our towns and countryside, our expectations of wealth.

The United States is in fact using more than half of the world's supply of fossil fuels. Sweden, a country with a comparable standard of living, uses one third less energy than the United States on a per capita basis. West Germany is also more economical. The average American's energy use is double that of the West German's for space heat and four times theirs for transportation. At the moment, oil imports are increasingly costly in terms of dollars and risk of armed conflict. Domestic oil is also more costly due to increasing scarcity and inaccessibility of deposits.

The Energy Crisis

Because of the scarcity of fossil fuels, there is an energy crisis. Fossil fuels were trees and plants when dinosaurs were on earth. They are non-renewable because the conditions that led to their formation will not return.

At the time of the earth's formation there weren't any plants and there was therefore no oxygen in the atmosphere. When plants did appear, so did oxygen, but for millions of years the level of atmospheric oxygen was low. There was not enough atmospheric oxygen to cause organic matter to decay as it would today, so dead plants and animals accumulated on the ground or on pond bottoms. They accumulated layer upon layer, and then were covered over by sediment and silt. The sediment became rock, and under this enormous weight the plants eventually became oil and natural gas and coal.

Given the growing scarcity and our national rate of consumption, we do have to stop and carefully consider how we use energy.

What is the government doing about the energy crisis?

Ideally, all efforts should be going into making the transition to energy systems based on renewable resources: sun, wind, water, plants. Unfortunately this isn't so. The government, the oil companies, and the military industry continue to subsidize nonrenewable resources.

Generally speaking, they are looking for equivalents to oil and gas: that is, fuel systems that will produce the same types of energy so that existing industries and institutions can remain intact, whether they make sense or not. Rather than investing in alternatives and renewables, the government and business have increased their investments in very expensive capital-intensive measures such as nuclear reactors. As we have seen in the section on nuclear power, this leads to heavy environmental consequences. But it is also an unwise economic strategy.

Those who favor nuclear power use the energy crisis to declare that, because we are running out of fossil fuels such as oil, coal, and natural gas, we must turn to nuclear power for our energy. There are several problems with this approach. One is that nuclear power can produce only one form of energy: electricity, which has only a limited number of efficient uses. In fact only eight percent of our energy use requires electricity. Other uses fulfilled by oil, such as home heating and gasoline for cars, cannot be replaced very efficiently by electricity. Another point is that nuclear power is based on uranium, another non-renewable commodity. Sooner or later we must face the fact that we cannot rely indefinitely on non-renewable fossil fuels and uranium.

Large power systems have become accepted as necessary for the amounts of energy we need today. However, there are technologies available now that could help make possible a shift to a solar-based society. A change away from centralized production of power does mean a shift from an attitude of dominating nature to one of integration with it, of adapting ourselves and our technologies to limited rather than abundant resources.

Ours isn't the first energy crisis. Throughout history people have treated easily available fuel supplies as though they would last forever. The Greeks and Romans hit hard times when the Mediteranean forests had been razed for firewood.

We are currently sliding down the back side of an energy boom, one that might eventually appear as an aberrant blip in our history. This descent, coupled with a strong incentive to find alternatives to nuclear power, has turned our attention to conservation and renewable resources as potential power sources. More and more communities are beginning to look to solar methods, windmills and hydro-electric power for heat and electricity. Seeming new, exotic, and very clever,it is surprising and wonderful to learn that these tools have been with us for centuries, their development interrupted periodically by "fast"fuels like oil.

Conservation is the important partner to small-scale energy systems. With oil and gas so cheap and abundant for so many years, there has been little incentive to conserve resources. However, as these fuel supplies have been dwindling, our dependence on them has been increasing. There are many more cars, trucks, and airplanes than there were in 1950, their growth in numbers encouraged through programs subsidized by the government, such as highway construction and airport expansion. Compatible support for conservation should help eliminate our need for oil imports as well as our need for nuclear reactors.

There are two basic ways to conserve. One is to use less energy by turning off lights, turning down thermostats, and driving less. The other is through technical efficiency, which means getting things to work better. Improved building design that uses passive solar heating and good insulation, adaptation of older buildings to make them heat-tight, the development of fuel-efficient transportation are the kinds of measures that could save enough fuel to eliminate all need for imported oil. A 1979 Harvard Business School report said that reducing present waste of energy will provide "the cheapest, safest, most productive energy alternative readily available in large amounts, the equivalent of the elimination of all imported oil . . . and then some!"

Appropriate Technologies: Conservation and Renewable Resources

What are these renewable energy systems and how do they work?

Passive solar: The sun's heat is admitted through southfacing windows or skylights. The building is designed to absorb and store the heat during the day and to release it gradually during the night.

Active solar: The sun heats air or water in collectors placed on a roof or south wall. "Active" systems rely on fans and pumps to distribute the heat.

Hydro-electric power: Dammed water is released to turn turbines, which generate electricity.

Biomass: This term includes wood, field crops and plant wastes, organic garbage, and manure. Most of these materials can be used for the production of heat and electricity.

Wind: The energy of the wind turns a shaft. This mechanical energy is converted into electricity by a generator.

Photovoltaic cells: These are solar cells that convert sunlight directly into electricity.

Energy is efficiently used when the quality of the energy source is matched to the quality of the task, or end-use. For example, electricity as a source of energy is efficient for turning a motor but very inefficient for providing heat. This matching process of the right quality of energy to the right quality of use determines whether a nation is using its energy supply efficiently or not. The other factor in good energy use is the extent to which energy is being wasted through improper production methods and inefficient usage because in transmission so much is lost to the air as low temperature heat.

A frequent argument against a solar economy is that we are not technically capable of it and don't have the time to develop it. This is not true. By tightening up our energy use, we could buy ourselves the time to develop a solar-based economy.

Solar energy is *the* primary energy source on earth. It makes life possible through plant growth, which is the basic food supply as well as the base for the atmosphere. The heating and cooling of the earth as the sun rises and sets creates the winds. Firewood, an indirect source of solar energy, has always been a fuel. And fossil fuels, once trees and plants, are stored solar energy.

There does not have to be an energy crisis as long as we choose to combine conservation with renewable resources. There is, literally, enough for everyone. New technologies are taking old tools and transforming them into more efficient and practical ones. Using renewable resources holds great promise for living in a balanced manner with enough energy for our needs, without causing pollution of air and water.

But if we need lots of energy, how can these little power systems help us? Look at how much power the "little" machines could provide:

—Active and passive solar systems could replace one million barrels of oil a day by the year 2000.

—Wind power could provide more power than we get from all U.S. nuclear power plants.

What about jobs?

We are in a transition period in which industries related to oil, steel, and automotive vehicles, for instance, are being hit hard. Inevitably some jobs will become obsolete, but that does not mean there will not be other jobs. With some imagination and planning, industries will have to make changes, or at least modify products so that they are efficient and make sense in present conditions. Could an automobile factory switch over to production of home electrical generators? Some bottle plants might close, but wouldn't there be a lot of jobs in recycling? Necessary weatherization of homes becomes a conservation industry. Nuclear power plants employ a lot of workers while they are being built, but all estimates show that solar energy employs many more.

In the fall of 1980, the first National Labor Conference for Safe Energy and Full Employment was held in Pittsburgh. Concerned about the dangers for nuclear workers and seeing the need to make a transition to renewable resource and conservation industries, the conference issued this statement:

> Let the word go out today to the nuclear industry and to the government that representatives of powerful unions met in conference and that we are determined to create a new social force that will throw its weight into the fight for safe energy and a full employment future.

At the same conference, Rosemary Trump, a union official, urged that labor movements reach out to natural allies such as women's and environmental groups. She said:

> We may not have the money the giant corporations have, but we have the people and the spirit. . . . We in the labor movement always understand that nothing comes easy. . . . But when we all work together, they've never stopped us.

Models for the Future

The transition from fossil fuels to renewables will be expensive. Not to make that transition will be even more expensive. One of the difficulties facing us is the cost of solar collectors and weatherization of old buildings. The cost will stay high as long as the government continues to subsidize oil. But all across the country people have gotten together in their communities to find ways to get off or cut down dependence on the oil/nukes power systems.

Somerville, Massachusetts, is just beginning to work out a plan for an energy transition. As in many other communities, income needed within the city is leaving to purchase energy for heat, electricity, transportation. The Citizens Energy Advisory Committee (CEAC), a broad coalition of residents and organizations, was formed with these goals:

—to involve the whole community in local energy planning: residents, business people, city workers;

—to determine how local reinvestment of energy dollars can best meet the needs of all Somerville residents;

—to encourage local and regional energy resources based on safe, affordable, and dependable energy options.

Working in cooperation with City Hall, community service organizations, area universities and local businesses, the Citizens Energy Advisory Committee has produced a comprehensive energy plan for Somerville which will help meet energy needs and therefore many of the economic needs of the community. Having completed the energy planning process, CEAC has now undertaken a more action-oriented project: the creation of a model for neighborhood energy-efficiency in Somerville.

Davis, California, is a community that has a well-established program combining conservation and solar energy. In 1968 the people of Davis decided to cut fuel costs and made an energy study of their city. The study eventually resulted in a series of city ordinances that regulated building construction, encouraged bike paths, provided for the planting of trees for summer shade and even called for greater use of clotheslines. Streets were narrowed and municipal cars and trucks were gradually replaced by compact models. Building codes ensure that all new housing be positioned on the building lot to take advantage of the sun's heat in winter and shade in summer. Good insulation is demanded by the regulations. As a result, electritcity use in Davis has dropped about eighteen percent.

As the perils of a nuclear society become clearer and the costs of an oil economy increase, choices will be forced upon us. Invention arises from necessity. These communities, and others like them, have begun seeking out connections that make sense in terms of energy and economy. The changes ahead for all of us could hopefully and inevitably bring us back to a balance within our societies and in relation to the earth. If we start to wonder about a peaceful, cooperative society, isn't that the beginning?

How would you answer if your child asked:

Kate: They sell things to make a profit. If they can sell something for more than it costs to make it, then they can keep the extra money. Big producers and their advertisers want us to buy their products—whether we need them or not—so then they can get the money.

Alice: Someone may have a good idea at one point with a wonderful invention, but in the end it's money. I suppose I should let them know about all the people who have jobs in all the factories, but I've basically talked about concentrated power and the fact that people really have lost sight of what's OK and what's not—we have been so over confident. We talk a lot about all sorts of products, toys, foods, pesticides, cigarettes, and how they're being sold. They can experiment with a few junk food items and cheap toys, and then contrast them with other food items and toys. And they know the difference. We really do live with two cultures (there are many cultures, but we all live with a disparity), and we choose to go with the livelier one. I think that lifts us above cynicism. As they get older, the conversations will of course become more complex. I'm trying to tune them into genuine connections now. What do we need? Is it good for us? Is it harmful or wasteful? Etc.

Hayat: There are many business people whose only interest is to get rich. They don't always care who they harm while making money. So even if they know the product is bad for you, they will advertise and try to convince you to buy it without worrying

"If it's not good for us, why do they try to sell it?"

very much about your health. It's up to you to outsmart the businessmen and not get taken in by their commercials, but instead always decide for yourself whether the product is worth buying or not. It's kind of like becoming detectives and sleuthing around ourselves.

Ellie: In this country, we have an economic system called capitalism. People try to make money by selling things to other people. Sometimes they forget that some things like lots of sugar or chemicals in food are bad for people, so they try to sell them to us. Sometimes, even if they aren't greedy, they try to sell us bad things because, if they don't they'll lose their jobs. It doesn't mean they are bad people—only that they are scared. We have to let them know that we don't want the bad things by not buying them. That way they'll try to sell us good things instead. Even better, we can learn to make lots of things ourselves. Daddy makes our bread, and next year we'll have a garden and grow some of our own food—that way we won't have to buy food with bad things in it. We also have to write letters to our Congresspeople and tell them we don't want bad things in our food or in the air, the earth, or the ocean, and tell them not to let people sell bad things.

Barbara: A business has to sell to go on. What do you think?

My daughter is six years old, and the problem of explaining evil is just now surfacing. Lately, she's been trying to reconcile what we tell her about products advertised on TV with the messages we've given her about lying and treating other people with love. "If it's bad for me, why do they try to sell it to me?" that question has come up a lot. I try to answer it by explaining that most people who work for advertisers aren't bad; they're doing their job and have lost touch with their responsibilities as people. They're not bad people, I tell her, only mistaken. I tell her that the advertisers have families to support and would lose their jobs if they didn't do what they were told to do to sell products. She struggles with it.

My husband and I may call the exploiters all kinds of names between ourselves, but not with her. I continue to try to humanize the face of evil with her, to try and impart something of the old Catholic concept of hating the sin but not the sinner. I figure that now we are approaching the time when she's going to start asking more difficult questions; she's starting to show deep concern about war and poor people.

Ellie

IV. Taking Action for the World We Want

Taking Action Toward Peace

Sooner or later, parents grappling with the huge, mind boggling realities of the nuclear world come to realize that political action has become a parental priority. As parents, we need to start doing the things that will make the world safer for us and our kids.

In this chapter, we present an overview of different kinds of political actions that people can take on a grassroots level. We do, as a group and as individuals, advocate political involvement as both an antidote to despair and a necessary part of parenting today.

We also believe that both grown-ups and children can use a little "good news," stories to tell each other in these dark days, to give each other hope and heart. This chapter is full of such stories and examples of everyday people taking actions aimed at eliminating the threats of both nuclear and "conventional" wars. We give examples of actions in our communities, our schools, and of different possibilities for involvement for people with varying amounts of time, energy and resources.

As children grow, they gain a sense of their power and its limitations. When children see adults using their power to change things for the better, they learn how to use their own youthful energy in positive and effective ways.

There are countless opportunities, large and small, for political action. The important thing is to find what we are comfortable with, because each and every individual effort makes a difference. Sometimes a simple communication between two people can have a tremendous impact. Talking to our friends and neighbors about our concerns is a political process that can have far-reaching results.

We hope this chapter will spark parents to come together to help build a huge and multi-faceted "human lobby" which will eventually turn society around. We can change the world, by placing the needs of the world's children at the center of our priorities.

History of the Anti-Nuclear Movement

Ever since the explosion of the first atomic bomb, there have been people expressing concern about its potential for world destruction. On December 10, 1945, Einstein addressed a Nobel anniversary dinner with a speech entitled "The War is Won, But the Peace is Not." A year later, Einstein reflected on the apathy of the general public in the face of this new and terrifying threat:

> Most people have lost courage and just continue to live their everyday lives; whether frightened or indifferent, they passively observe the ghastly tragi-comdey which is being played, for all to see, on the international stage where, under bright lights, actors perform their appointed roles. . . .
> "The fact that men have become accustomed to war preparations has so corrupted their mentality that objective and humane thinking becomes a virtual impossibility; such thinking will even be regarded as suspect and will be suppressed as unpatriotic."[1]

Dissent was suppressed as unpatriotic in the fifties, when U.S. Senator Joseph McCarthy and his supporters labeled almost any objection to government policy "COMMUNISM." (This practice, called "red-baiting," continues today.)

In the fifties, individuals and groups began to protest atomic testing in the atmosphere. As organizations like Women Strike for Peace and SANE alerted the public to the dangers of radioactive fallout, people became increasingly alarmed. Finally in 1963, under world pressure, the U.S. and the U.S.S.R. signed the Limited Nuclear Test Ban Treaty, outlawing above-ground testing.

Early successes in the anti-nuclear-power struggle included a stunning blow to the nuclear industry in 1962. Citizen activists forced Consolidated Edison to cancel plans for a nuclear reactor in Queens, New York. A plant on Oregon's coast was defeated by referendum in 1966.

During the sixties, people in the United States participated in national dialogue about the politics and morality of the Vietnam War. The country went through a wrenching social upheaval, and many Americans experienced a painful political awakening. In the late sixties, anti-nuclear forces, religious groups, and others dedicated to peace joined opponents of Third World intervention to form the largest popular anti-war movement in the history of the United States.

Throughout the seventies, public sophistication in the area of nuclear weapons grew dramatically. With no end (or THE END) to the arms race in sight, the world-wide disarmament movement was beginning to find its strength.

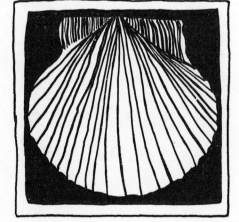

In 1976 and 1977 a series of civil disobedience actions at Seabrook, New Hampshire, brought huge numbers of people together, made the anti-nuclear movement an organized and growing national phenomenon, and brought the general public's attention to the issues of nuclear power. This movement, plus the impetus of the Three Mile Island accident, brought one hundred thousand people to the lawns of the Capital in Washington, D.C., in April 1979. They all said "No Nukes!"

In the fall of 1981 millions of Europeans demonstrated in protest of the arms race, and at the roles of the U.S. and the Soviet Union in threatening world security. And on June 12, 1982, hundreds of thousands of Americans travelled to New York City's Central Park to demonstrate their desire for peace. Joined by people from many other countries, demonstrators amazed the country with their numbers (too many for an accurate count) and the peacefulness of their action.

"Don't Mourn, Organize!"

Whatever the focus of the movement, it is clear that nuclear power and nuclear weapons are intimately connected. To fight against one is to fight against the other, and uniting the two struggles gives us added strength. By becoming aware of the links between these two industries, we are also make aware of further connections. The machinery that sets in motion the uncaring policies of nuclear power and nuclear weapons is also uncaring about environmental policies, water quality regulations, hazardous waste clean-up programs, or health and safety regulations for workplaces.

As we make these connections, we expose the lie that we are all separate individuals forced by "human nature" to fight each other endlessly for scarce resources. We can see that valuable and abundant resources are being stolen from us and destroyed for the benefit of a few. As our resistance strengthens and grows, it becomes clearer that racial and sexual hatred and other forms of prejudice get in the way of effective action.

As difficult as it is sometimes, we must continue to uncover the relationships between nuclear weapons, nuclear power, environmental destruction, and the social cancers of racism, sexism, and class exploitation. These connections are like pieces of a complex puzzle. The meaning of the puzzle becomes clearer and clearer as more connections are made. The closer we come to the solution, the closer we are to the powerful solidarity we need to build lasting peace and security.

Washing one's hands of the conflict between the powerful and the powerless means to side with the powerful, not to be neutral.
Paulo Freire

Peace Action at the Grassroots: The Cambridge Peace Education Project

The following discussion, excerpted from an article by Hap Tierney, member of the Cambridge Peace Education Project, highlights the exciting development of citizen involvement and action:

In the wake of the growing grassroots opposition to the continuing arms buildup, city leaders in Cambridge, Massachusetts, took unprecedented action, doing what governing bodies are supposed to do: protect the lives and welfare of the citizens they are elected to serve. On September 9, 1981, the Cambridge city council announced to the city and to the world the publication and distribution to all Cambridge households of a ten-page brochure, *Cambridge and Nuclear Weapons: Is There a Place to Hide?* The brochure clearly states and explains the councilors' belief that "the sole means of protecting Cambridge citizens from nuclear warfare would be for nations with nuclear arms to destroy those arms and renounce their use."

The brochure received immediate national and international acclaim. Media from Europe to Japan carried the story; the city council was flooded with grateful thanks, some with money, all requesting from one copy to two thousand copies for further distribution. Widely publicized and discussed in Cambridge, the brochure surely influenced the results of a referendum in which 17,979 Cambridge voters (seventy percent of those voting on the question) supported a freeze of further development of nuclear weapons in Cambridge.

The city council apparently touched a nerve of apprehension and alarm in Cambridge and throughout the country. Like rain in the desert, it has been received eagerly by many who have been waiting for *somebody* to do *something*. How did it all begin?

In early 1981, as the Reagan administration's war rhetoric mounted, the state Civil Defense Agency, following instructions from the Federal Emergency Management Agency, sent to Cambridge a number of copies of 'Relocation Instructions, Greater Boston Area, Suburban West."(As the home of the Draper Laboratory, where ICBM guidance systems are designed, and MIT, the nation's second largest university recipient of Pentagon research dollars, Cambridge is considered by many to be a prime target for a nuclear attack.) Cambridge officials were instructed to develop a local component of the plan, allocating fire, police and medical personnel and supplies, and alerting and familiarizing Cambridge residents with the evacuation plan.

The plan developed by the state Civil Defense Agency instructs Cambridge residents, upon official notification of impending attack, to leave Cambridge and drive one hundred miles across the state on Route 2 to Greenfield, Massachusetts, taking with them survival supplies and 'important papers,' including credit cards and stocks and bonds.

It may have been the credit cards, or it may have been the thought of all of Cambridge cramming on to Route 2, badly congested with an ordinary day's traffic, or it may have been the fact that in a low income city like Cambridge, there are many households without cars. Whatever it was, when the plan reached the City Councilors, several of them reacted with disbelief, dismay or anger. 'I thought it was a comic book," says Councilor (and State Representative) Saundra Graham, "except that it wasn't funny."

Several Councilors placed the civil defense plan on the Council agenda and called for a public hearing to take testimony from all interested parties on the nuclear threat to Cambridge and the pros and cons of civil defense. On March 9, the City Council heard impassioned anti-nuclear testimony from Cambridge residents and area scientists, including Dr. Helen Caldicott of Physicians for Social Responsibility, and the late George Kistiakowsky, one of the designers of the first atomic bomb, later science advisor to President Eisenhower, and president of the Council for a Livable World. Proponents of the civil defense "relocation" plan were also heard, but the disarmament advocates clearly carried the day.

A week later, Councilor David Wylie introduced a resolution which said in part:

WHEREAS:
The only conclusion which could be reached from the testimony was that the sole means of protecting Cambridge citizens from nuclear warfare would be for nations with nuclear arms to destroy those arms and renounce their use: and . . . now therefore be it
ORDERED:
That the City Manager is requested to direct the Civil Defense Director of Cambridge to hold in abeyance further distribution of the regional evacuation plan and immediately to prepare and distribute to all Cambridge citizens before the City Council recesses for the summer a publication which would describe why no step short of nuclear disarmament by all nations could protect Cambridge citizens against a nuclear war, drawing upon the testimony presented on March 9 regarding the number, variety, and destructive power of nuclear arms. . . .

The resolution passed 8 to 0. At a continued hearing the following week, the Council passed another resolution, calling for public education on nuclear warfare and for an anti-nuclear educational program in the city's schools.

A group of local citizens, determined that the ideas expressed in the resolution not be lost or diluted, quickly coalesced as the Cambridge Peace Education Project (CPEP) and offered its support and assistance to the City Council. CPEP was literally born on the stairway leading down from the Council chamber as that meeting broke up. It began with four or five people and grew rapidly to a membership of over 30.

It soon became clear that both the city officials and citizen's group were serious. A Cambridge lawyer with training in both physics and technical writing was hired by the City Manager to write a new brochure which would present to Cambridge residents the information that had so impressed the Councilors at the public hearing. CPEP met and drew up its own outline for the brochure. The group felt strongly that in addition to focusing on the realities of nuclear war and emphasizing the conclusions that there is no defense, the brochure must focus on the options for citizen action, describe what the average citizen can do, and include a list of local peace groups that citizens might join.

In addition to the brochure committee a second CPEP group was also getting underway, a 'curriculum' committee, composed primarily of teachers, to work with the public schools in developing a peace curriculum. In mid-April, shortly after passage of the City Council resolutions, the school Committee had passed its own order, directing the school superintendent to:

Initiate and work with community groups to develop an appropriate peace curriculum throughout the grades that supports children's and young people's understanding of the history, scientific backgrounds, economics and politics of waging peace in the nuclear age.

CPEP defined its role as one of support and assistance to the school system and to individual teachers rather than as being responsible for the curriculum itself. Committee members felt it important not to impose their own ideas and not to add to the work of classroom teachers. CPEP would serve as a resource and support system and help develop staff leadership and peace activities. Suggestions for CPEP's role included collecting resource materials, setting up a speaker's bureau, working with libraries to develop peace bibliographies, arranging coffee hours for teachers, and political action in the November election.

Both of these committees continued throughout the summer of '81: the Curriculum Committee to contact Cambridge teachers and to develop strategies for getting information to them; the Brochure Committee to follow and oversee development of the brochure, step by step, to its final form. As the brochure neared completion, this committee gradually took on responsibility for publicity and outreach. CPEP agreed to do the publicity leg work: organize a press conference, write the press release, and make follow-up phone calls. Efforts were made to reach national as well as local media; newspapers, TV and radio stations, campus publications, national news magazines and progressive publicatons were all contacted.

The ensuing publicity more than rewarded CPEP's efforts. National Public Radio's *All Things Considered* recognized the importance of the Cambridge action and carried the story on their evening broadcast. Response to the broadcast has been a testament both to the program and to the Cambridge action: a lot of people were listening and a lot of them cared. Cards and letters from listeners have poured into the Cambridge City Council with praise and thanks. The Boston Globe carried the story prominently the next day and enthusiastically endorsed the Cambridge action in an editorial several days later. Other media, not present at the original press conference, picked up the story and it gradually spread around the world. Friends have sent articles from papers in California, Europe, Japan, and many places in between. Requests continue to come in and brochures to be sent out. CPEP members have hand carried them to Russia and shared them with visitors from Russia and Japan.

CPEP also planned other activities to heighten public awareness of the brochure and to generate as much discussion about the brochure and nuclear issues as possible. The City Council was asked, and agreed, to proclaim "Peace Month" in Cambridge. Contacts were made with local peace groups to alert and inform them of the city's action and to enlist their help in getting word out. After considerable discussion CPEP decided that a series of small neighborhood events would be more effective and reach more people than one larger, more spectacular event which might attract only those already committed to the disarmament cause. The group decided a "traveling slide show" would be the best means of bringing the message to the neighborhoods. After reviewing a number of slide shows CPEP chose *The War Nobody Wins,* produced by SANE, as meeting their criteria: accurate and informative, and not too long, not too technical and not too frightening. *Children of Hiroshima*, a short but powerful slide show based on writings and drawings of Hiroshima survivors and assembled by Peggy Schirmer, a member of both CPEP and Concerned Educators Allied for a Safe Environment (CEASE) and Linda De Lissovoy of CEASE, was chosen as an alternate.

CPEP then decided to add a few introductory pictures of Cambridge to go along with the slide shows as a further tie-in to the community, and a couple of members went off to take pictures around the city. The unexpected result was a seven minute professional quality slide show, *The Whole World in Our Hands*, put together by CPEP member Wattie Taylor. The slide show depicts a typical day in Cambridge and the doings of the ordinary people who live and work here, then contrasts this with the horrors of Hiroshima and asks "Could this happen here?" After reiterating the facts and anti-nuclear message of the brochure and why the City Council had it published, the focus moves to what the ordinary citizens can do, illustrating steps that anyone can take, and gently urging viewers to talk to friends, write letters to Washington, join in group activities and demonstrations, vote for peace-mongering candidates. Other CPEP members developed a study guide to accompany the slide show, with additional information and suggestions for action.

To all of CPEP's efforts the response has been overwhelmingly positive and supportive. It's clear that significant numbers of people within Cambridge and around the country apparently share the belief of CPEP members that the Cambridge City Council action was if not a true giant step, at least a small and important step for mankind. But it is only a beginning. Many more must follow before any of us are truly safe.[2]

Some More Action Suggestions

KNOXVILLE, Tennessee (UPI) - A cylinder of radioactive tritium, which can be used as nuclear bomb component, was lost yesterday from a truck that was taking it from Oak Ridge National Laboratory to an airport for shipment to Boston.

State radiological health director Mike Mobley said officials believe someone found the 36-inch-long footlocker containing the cylinder on the side of the road and kept it.

"It's not a good thing to lose," said Health Department spokeswoman Ann Stringham. "it is a very serious irritant. It will just about destroy throat and nasal passages if it is inhaled. There are also long-term health effects," she said.

The white fiberglass-paneled footlocker was labeled "Radioactive."

"Think globally, act locally!"

- Gather a group of friends together for a discussion. We can help educate ourselves and others through informal talks about issues of mutual concern.

- Help your school group get involved in promoting peace and understanding. Groups can sponsor a film or a speaker for their members and the public. Sometimes such educational meetings can be used to raise funds for other peace activities.

- Write letters to politicians, lawmakers, newspapers—let them know you are there, that you have an opinion, that your opinion matters. It has been proven again and again that public pressure is effective—it *can* make changes happen!

- Get involved in community activities. Find out how your tax dollars are spent. (Remember the world spends a billion a day on arms. As Thomas Jefferson once said, "The care of human life and happiness, and not their destruction, is the first and only legitimate object of good government.") Does your community need more day care centers, improved educational services, better housing, pollution controls, a toxic waste clean-up?

- Find out what the kids are learning in school. You have the right to know, and most teachers will welcome your concern and involvement. Share peace education resources with teachers, your school committee, the PTA, and other groups.

- Check out your local city politics. You may have more support than you realize. Many groups have been surprised at how much influence they have on issues such as transportation of waste through the community. Our presence at town or city council meetings and public hearings can be a critical factor whenever decisions are made.

- Community groups often form around specific issues. Do some investigating. Is there a research facility near you, releasing hazardous gases or improperly disposing of wastes? Are toxic substances being transported through your community? Tell others—sound the alarm. The only way we're going to save the planet from environmental catastrophe is to identify the sources of contamination and start to clean them up, right now, community by community.

- Demonstrations and rallies are often a good place to get information and support. Depending on the nature of the demonstration, such events can be a high-energy place for children, and very strengthening. As one long-time activist put it, "My kids have always acted like they had a handle on the nuclear issue. I think it's because their first contact with the whole subject was the mass civil disobedience movement at Seabrook in 1977. It made them feel so strong to see *'so* many people against the bad nukes'."

Many issues can be raised in unique ways through drama and ritual. Group acting and ceremony have a powerful impact on both viewers and participants. In October 1982, thousands of Swedes joined hands and formed a four-mile-long "human bridge for peace" between the U.S. and the Soviet embassies.

Another very effective dramatic group action is called a "die-in." A large number of people are gathered in a public place and a siren is blown. As the siren sounds, people slowly "drop dead" where they are standing, until finally all that is visible is a sea of "dead" bodies. With the siren wailing in the background, it can be a chilling reminder of nuclear death. The die-in has been used to demonstrate the effects of the neutron bomb (The buildings are left standing as the people "die"). In one Japanese die-in, four hundred thousand people lay down on the ground as if dead, in protest at the nuclear arms race between the U.S. and the Soviet Union.

In November 1980 and again in 1981, several thousand women visited the Pentagon and took part in an unusual demonstration. The Women's Pentagon Action combined ritual and theater with protest and non-violent civil disobedience. Both demonstrations included a slow, silent march through Arlington National Cemetery, and the creation of a symbolic cemetery on the parade ground in front of the Pentagon. As one participant described it,

> The headstones we planted in the ground were memorials to sisters, mothers and daughter victimized by violence. Some of us mourned silently and many of us cried as we read the inscriptions—Yolanda Ward . . . Karen Silkwood . . . Anna Mae Aquash . . . My Mother. Died of Cancer. 1929—1979 . . .Marie Valdez. Died of a Coat-Hanger Abortion. 1963 . . . The unknown Woman . . . There were hundreds of them.
>
> Grief turned to anger. We encircled the Pentagon, passing yarn and long stripes of cloth hand over hand, winding a braid that stretched around the massive 5-sided building. Then some women began to block the entrances by sitting down in front of the doors. Others wove brightly colored webs of yarn and material across building entrances. Men in fancy uniforms trying to get in heard women calling out, "Think about your children, your grandchildren!" and "Shame, shame". On this day, colonels and generals who are planning our annihilation were forced by our webs and our bodies to slow down, meet our eyes, hear our voices. "No more amazing inventions for death."
>
> It was a colorful and visually dramatic demonstration. I was glad there were photographers and film-makers (many from other countries) to record the Action. Words can't describe the evocative power of the rituals and costumes and banners, the imagination and pagentry of thousands of women participating in feminist street theatre.[3]

We want the uranium left in the earth and the earth given back to the people who tilled it. We want a system of energy which is renewable, which does not take resources out of the earth without returning them. We want those systems to belong to the people and their communities, not to the giant corporations which invariably turn knowledge into weaponry. We want the sham of Atoms for Peace ended, all nuclear plants decommissioned and the construction of new plants stopped. That is another war against the people and the child to be born in fifty years.

We want an end to the arms race. No more bombs. No more amazing inventions for death.

We understand all is connectedness. The earth nourishes us as we with our bodies will eventually feed it. Through us, our mothers connected the human past to the human future. We know the life and work of animals and plants in seeding, reseeding and in fact simply inhabiting this planet. Their exploitation and the organized destruction of never to be seen again species threatens and sorrows us.

With that sense, that ecological right, we oppose the financial connections between the Pentagon and the multinational corporations and banks that the Pentagon serves.

These connections are made of gold and oil. We are made of blood and bone, we are made of the sweet and finite resource, water.

We will not allow these violent games to continue. If we are here in our stubborn thousands today, we will certainly return in the hundreds of thousands in the months and years to come.

We know there is a healthy sensible loving way to live and we intend to live that way in our neighborhoods and our farms in these United States and among our sisters and brothers in all the countries of the world.

Excerpt from the Women's Pentagon
Action Unity Statement, 1982[4]

Peace Marchers

We can all, children and adults, take action in our own communities. A special event can be the source of many activities. Peace marchers led by Japanese Buddhist monks and nuns, passing through Boston en route to the U.N. Special Session on Disarmament, became the catalyst for parents, teachers, and children at Cambridge Friends School. A reception had been planned for the marchers, and Friends School wanted to participate in the welcome. Teachers felt enthusiastic about the children meeting people who are devoting their lives to disarmament and started planning peace activities.

But questions arose: What do children know about war, peace, and especially nuclear war? Are they worried? What information do parents want teachers to give and in what context? At a parent-teacher meeting arranged to discuss these questions, parents spoke of growing up in isolation with their fear about nuclear war. They wondered how they could confirm children's fears and offer support at the same time.

The preparations at school to welcome the peace marchers offered a chance to confirm the danger many young children suspect as well as the opportunity to participate with others in working toward peace and disarmament. The children made two large peace banners, decorated with trees and hearts and hands. Third and fourth graders folded one thousand paper cranes as an expression of their hopes for peace. A K-2 class made a book of drawings and writings about peace. On the evening of the reception, parents, teachers, and children joined the marchers with the banners they had made; paper cranes were given out to everyone at the gathering. At school the next day, the K-2 class presented their book to a visiting monk and nun and more cranes were given to them to pass out on the way to New York.

During the weeks of preparation, the children had been given a chance to ask questions about war and what had happened at Hiroshima. They had learned something about the peace movement. They had met extraordinary as well as ordinary people concerned about the future of the world. They had made peace "gifts" to be shared with many others. Parents had begun to voice their worries to each other and to seek out actions of their own. In helping the children, many were helped.

I felt very fortunate to have been a part of this project. So much news is bad: wars, fires, destruction. My nine-year-old doesn't want to hear any more! Here was a chance to connect with real people who are part of a real and very large international movement. Actual good news. It felt empowering to me to act with other adults for our children.

Alice

Recently Hsuan's teacher read her third and fourth grade class Sadako and the Thousand Cranes. *Sadako was born in Hiroshima in 1943 and died of leukemia in 1955. Reading the book was part of a spring peace education project to help the kids focus on the reason for the peace march and the U.N. Special session on Disarmament in June.*

Hsuan told me about the reading and as she did I had the impression that it had been a strengthening experience for her and the class. She said, "I just admire that girl (Sadako) so much. She was so brave. She was just so determined not to die. She did die, but she had so much courage."

Hsuan said that she and several other children cried all through the silent meeting that followed. Later, the class decided that they would fold one thousand paper cranes to present to the peace marchers. (The cranes symbolize longevity. Sadako had tried, and failed, to fold one thousand cranes so that the gods would restore her health.)

But then Hsuan said, "Why did we do such an awful thing? Why did we drop that bomb?"

I said, "We didn't; you didn't and I didn't."

I said there were people in the U.S. military and government who made that decision. But I couldn't answer the basic *why: How did people choose to use such a weapon? This could have been a long discussion. I was thinking of our contemporary responsibility, but I sensed Hsuan had had enough.*

Alice

Sample Letter to Parents:

Dear Parents,

Today the second grade group met together and we read Sadako and the Thousand Paper Cranes. *This is a true story about a Japanese girl who is a victim of the atom bomb sickness (leukemia). She died in 1955 and the story describes very movingly and beautifully the freedom of the spirit after death and how that spirit lives on to bring hope to new generations. A statue of Sadako holding a golden crane was built in her memory in Hiroshima Peace Park after children and young people throughout the country collected enough money for the project. Every year on 6 August, the Japanese celebrate Peace Day and children deliver a thousand paper cranes to her statue. They make a wish too. Their wish is engraved on the statue:*

This is our cry,

This is our prayer,

Peace in the world.

It is a stirring story and the children may want to talk some more about it with you. This week the Peace Walkers are arriving in Boston and we will be talking a lot about peace and what contributions we can make. If you have any ideas or want to talk with me about it, please contact me.

Yours,
Lynette

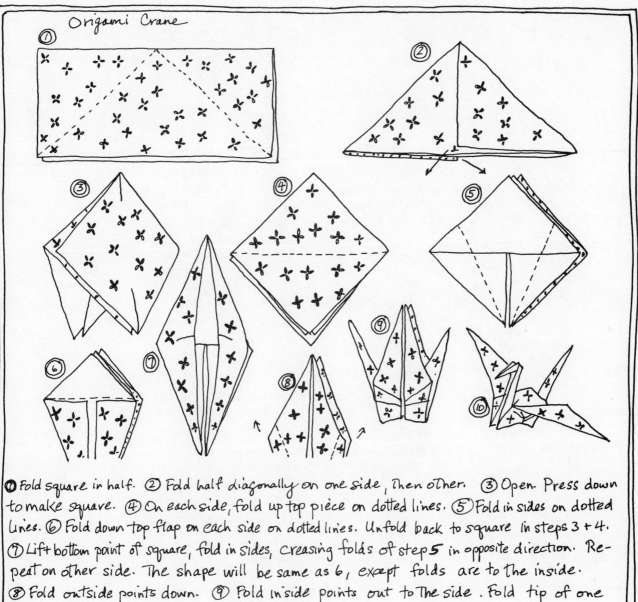

Origami Crane

① Fold square in half. ② Fold half diagonally on one side, then other. ③ Open. Press down to make square. ④ On each side, fold up top piece on dotted lines. ⑤ Fold in sides on dotted lines. ⑥ Fold down top flap on each side on dotted lines. Unfold back to square in steps 3 + 4. ⑦ Lift bottom point of square, fold in sides, creasing folds of step 5 in opposite direction. Repeat on other side. The shape will be same as 6, except folds are to the inside. ⑧ Fold outside points down. ⑨ Fold inside points out to the side. Fold tip of one point down for the head. ⑩ Fold wings up.

How would you answer if your child asked:

"Well, the U.S. is the best country, isn't it?"

Kate: We've always taught Ned that there's a difference between U.S. people and U.S. government. He knows that the U.S. government has done some shameful things, and that many people object and protest each time. Still, at ten years old, he wants to be proud of his country.

Alice: In actual fact, I don't think I've ever heard that one but if I did I would ask why she had said that. It could take the form of a long explanation through various aliens (humans as well as Star Wars and E.T. types), cultural differences, etc. I would probably be aware of this idea over a long period of time and find ways of weaving it into conversations. It's hard for me to be very succinct on this one.

Hayat: The people who live in the U.S. have good qualities and bad qualities just like people anywhere in the world, but the U.S. is so powerful and rich that it has ended up acting like a "bully" towards other countries. Many people in the U.S. do not feel that their government's actions are good or represent them, so many of us protest the actions of the U.S. government.

Ellie: We have lots of wonderful things here, that's true. We can vote and elect leaders of our choice and we can speak out about things we don't like. In lots of countries, people can't do those things. But that doesn't mean we are the best country. It's a big, big world and there are lots of countries and lots of different ways that people live. It always seems like your country is the best. It's good that you like living here—it's good that you like living where you are—but it doesn't mean it's the best country.

Barbara: It's our country. Any country can be improved. I'd like to see it better. Do you think it's best? How would you like to see it better?

A group walk on a particular theme is a good way to promote public awareness and education. A large number of people walking together with banners and leaflets can be a vehicle for stirring interest in an issue and reaching many with the information.

Some walks are very long and take months to organize. One such walk was the Continental Walk for Disarmament and Social Justice, 1976, from the West Coast to the East Coast, publicizing the need for arms reduction. There have been some international walks for disarmament, including one from the U.S. to the Soviet Union.

Small-scale walks are also effective. In 1978, a number of people who did not wish to participate in a civil disobedience action at the Seabrook power plant in New Hampshire planned a walk as an alternative action. It was a week-long event called the Boston to Seabrook Safe Energy Walk.

The planning for the walk began with a large mailing to all the towns along the route, to see who wished to become part of the organizing network. Mailing lists were obtained from local peace and anti-nuclear groups. People who responded from the same towns were connected up with each other and small committees were formed in each town,

One of the main benefits of the walk was that grassroots organizing was initiated all along the route. The walkers handed out thousands of leaflets in towns and neighborhoods where the nuclear issue had not been a major topic of concern.

Walking to Build Awareness

There have been several successful—and inspiring—referenda campaigns in various states. Issues are brought to the fore by making them the subject of questions to be voted on by the entire electorate. A great deal of organizing is being done on two major nuclear issues: waste disposal and a nuclear weapons freeze. In 1980, despite industry opposition, three out of six referenda on nuclear power and waste in different states were passed by voters and became law. Your state may have referenda campaigns on nuclear issues. Try to find out about these and support them. If there is no such drive in your state, organizing a referendum would be a tremendous achievement.

Referendum Campaigns

Massachusetts Nuclear Referendum Campaign

The Massachusetts Nuclear Referendum Campaign brought the issue of nuclear waste disposal and nuclear plant construction to the ballot in November, 1982. Specifically, the referendum required that before any new nuclear waste dumps or power plants could be authorized for construction, the Legislature would have to certify that certain environmental, economic and safety standards had been met. The project would then have to be approved by a majority of the voters in a statewide referendum.

The idea originated in 1980, when some citizens got together because they were concerned about the lack of legislative initiative and citizen involvement in decisions about nuclear power. Informal discussions led to a three-part strategy involving research on referendum drives in other states, an exploration of the relevant legal issues, and a telephone survey of voter attitudes in the state.

After drafting a four-page ballot initiative, submitting it to the Massachusetts Attorney General, and fulfilling a statutory requirement that over 58,868 signatures of registered voters in favor of the petition be collected in a two-month period, the petition qualified for the ballot in the November 1982 election.

Sixty-eight percent of the voters in Massachusetts approved the measure—over 1.2 million people—and it became a state statute having the weight of law.

For more information on the Nuclear Referendum Committee contact Amy Goldsmith, P.O. Box 1712, Boston, MA 02205.

Following this success, organizers in Cambridge again placed a referendum on the November, 1983 ballot—this time a proposal for a "Nuclear-Free Cambridge" that would have outlawed nuclear weapons research and development work in Cambridge.

> *The key section stated: "No person, corporation, university, laboratory, institution or other entity shall, within the City of Cambridge, engage in work the purpose of which is the research, development, testing, evaluation, production, maintenance, storage, transportation, and-or disposal of nuclear weapons or the components of nuclear weapons."*
>
> *The Philadelphia Inquirer*
> November 12, 1983

The Nuclear Free Cambridge Act would have outlawed research, manufacture and storage of nuclear weapons systems within the city limits. The Campaign was the first time a city with operating nuclear weapons firms had tried to ban them, and it attracted national and international attention.

Voters favored a Nuclear Free Cambridge when the campaign began, and when the votes were counted, the measure lost only by a margin of 17,331 (59.7%) to 11,677 (40.3%).

An expensive public relations campaign, launched by Draper Laboratories, made the difference, according to Nuclear Free Cambridge organizer Richard Schreuer. Draper, which has $140 million in Defense Department contracts, hired two public relations consultants to organize opposition to the measure. Money poured into Massachusetts to finance the counter-campaign from such companies as Hughes Aircraft, General Electric and the Sperry Corporation of New York.[5] Cambridge voters were contacted by mail and phone, sometimes to the point of harrassment, about the "dangers" of the measure. Schreuer figures that the opposition spent an unprecedented total of $507,000 to defeat the measure (that's $17.50 a vote), in contrast to the $20,000 spent by the Nuclear Free Cambridge campaign.

Despite the defeat, organizers see the campaign as a step forward for the nuclear free movement. Over one hundred cities and towns across the country are working on establishing nuclear free zones, and Nuclear Free Cambridge is ready to help by sharing what they've learned. Resource packets on establishing nuclear free zones are available from the Boston Mobilization for Survival office (see organization list).

The actions described here have inspired the five of us to take our own action in the form of this support book. There are countless other efforts by people in the U.S. and all over the world, to turn our direction towards wholeness and life.

You may have an action to share, so we can all learn from each other. Be of good cheer. Tell you children about *people's energy* and that we are all a part of that!

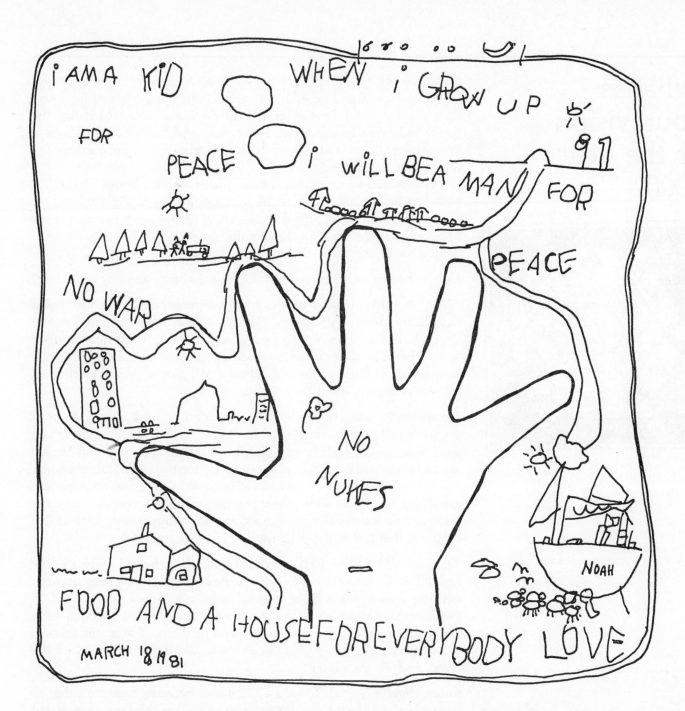

V. Visions of the Children

What is your vision of the year 2000?

Maya (eleven years): Well, it really won't be like my vision. I think all the houses should be solar-powered. I saw a magnificent house on Razz ma Tazz. All three sides and the roof was covered by dirt; the fourth side was facing towards the sun, and the whole side was a greenhouse! On top of the roof was a windmill to supply energy for the rest of the house.

There would be no nuclear power plants. I don't know what to do with the waste. We have to have a committee to figure this out. Everyone should have jobs and we should throw away the computers so people can do the jobs that computers do now. The more money people have, the more they should give away.

Hayat: You mean everyone should have the same amount of money?

Maya: No, Mummy, people can have different amounts, but if you have more money you should have to give away more money, and if you have less money then you shouldn't have to give any money at all. There should be a fair government to figure all this out. It should be made up of fair women and fair men. All people should be allowed to believe any religion they want.

Taras (nine years): If you want my opinion, what it's going to be is disgusting! If I were president, I would try to stop nuclear power and stuff that upsets wildlife and get things fair in the male and female sex and give food to people who need food to stop them from starving. As you can see I don't believe in violence. While we and other people are sitting in comfortable places wanting more and complaining, the poor people who really need more are not complaining. One of my fantastic theories is if we could live like the hobbits!

Toby (eleven years): I know what I'd like it to be but I don't know how it's really going to be. I want it to be all peace, no fighting between nations. I want there to be a good economy for all the nations. In parts of Africa that don't have enough food, I want them to have enough money for food and clothes and medicine. I want the schools to have enough money. No nuclear war, air to be clean and all the rivers and all the water.

Karen (twelve years): There's a difference between how it's going to be and how I'd like it to be. It's going to be polluted and maybe mutated from radiation. How I'd like it to be is a pollution-free world in which there is no radiation and everyone has enough money for all the necessities and luxuries of life. I would like it to be a totally solar and geothermal world.

Ned (eleven years): In the year 2000 I hope there is no pollution, no need for police, no need for any armies, fresh water, nobody starving. When I close my eyes I see automatic everything. You could take an elevator from the apartment to the corner store, sort of like a moving sidewalk. Even if it wasn't everywhere, with modern technology, it could happen in some cities. There would be no president and no vice-president. People would make their own decisions by a vote, the majority would decide.

Deidre (six years): **I would like to know lowercase and big case letters. I'd like to see deers and bears and birds singing in the forest. I'd like flowers and trees outside and lots of trash in bags, no litter. If I close my eyes I see a rainbow and a heart under it and lots of people walking around giving love to one another.**

Samantha (six years): **I would like a world with green grass and, instead of flowers, hearts growing! Hearts are pretty and nice. Everbody is nice and there are no bad people like robbers and kidnappers. I wish it was never nighttime. I get scared sometimes in the nighttime. I wish it was always Christmas!**

Hsuan (ten years): **When I grow up I would like the world to be like a UNICEF puzzle with everyone holding hands . . . everyone joining hands from every nation. I would like everyone to forget they were enemies. I want presidents and everyone to realize that weapons aren't any good. And that's all.**

Hui-min (six years): **I'd like there to be three worlds: one with peace, one medium with nuclear power plants, and one that doesn't have peace at all, so people can have a choice of which world they'd like to be in. If they wanted to risk being in a war and getting killed, they could. In the second world they could have nuclear power and lots of candy and fights. In the third world they can have peace totally. I want to live in the third world.**

These words are reminders that we owe a debt to our children and their children. At a conference in Boston on "Families and the Nuclear Crisis,"Dr. Eric Chivian of International Physicians for the Prevention of Nuclear War quoted the following Kenyan proverb:

Treat the earth well; it was not given to you by your parents. It was loaned to you by your children.

Part I The Heart of the Matter

PARENTING FOR POSSIBILITY

1. Dr. John Mack, "The Psychosocial Effects of the Nuclear Arms Race," *Bulletin of the Atomic Scientists*, April 1981, p. 18-23.
2. Ibid.
3. One good resource is *A Manual on Nonviolence and Children* edited by Stephanie Judson (Philadelphia: New Society Publishers, 1984). This book includes "For the Fun of It! Selected Cooperative Games for Children and Adults" by Marta Harrison and the Nonviolence and Children Program.
4. There has been far too little research into the roots of violence in our culture, but at last we seem to have some solid evidence that what we do as parents has much to do with what our society becomes. A study reported by James W. Prescott in *The Bulletin of the Atomic Scientists* indicates a strong link between authoritarian, sexually repressive family structures and violent, militaristic societies.

    "Body Pleasure and the Origins of Violence" analyses a unique cross-cultural survey which puts together the results of all previously published major anthropological studies, and so is independent of the bias of any particular researcher. Four hundred different sources from around the world were compiled to find which cultural traits correlated with others. The result is a personality profile of societies, and gives us a chance to see the striking child-rearing differences between violent cultures and loving ones.

    The trait "high infant physical affection" by itself gives a 73 percent predictability of a low rate of adult physical violence in a culture. As a whole, those cultures which had the least occurence of interpersonal violence and militarism were the ones which displayed all of the following characteristics: late weaning, high infant physical affection, low incidence of infant punishment, and a high acceptance of sexual pleasure. Other traits of these cultures included low rate of theft, low religious activity, and low invidious display of wealth.

    On the other hand, cultures which exhibit any one of the following traits are likely to exhibit all or most of them: high rate of forcible personal crime, high incidence of theft, inferior status of women, punishment of extramarital sex, attempts to prevent young from engaging in sex, high castration anxiety, high sexual disability, and high incidence of killing, torturing and mutilating the enemy.

    Says Prescott, "These findings overwhemingly support the thesis that deprivation of body pleasure throughout life—but particularly during the formative periods of infancy, childhood and adolescence—is very closely related to the amount of warfare and interpersonal violence."

    (Verner, Robin, "Parenting Styles and Violent Cultures", *The Family Newsletter*, Vol. 3, No. 4, Box 225, Hardwick, Mass. 01037.)
5. PAD, PO Box 833, Brookline Village, MA 02147.
6. Ken Keyes, Jr., *The Hundredth Monkey* (St. Mary, KY: Vision Books, 1982)

DEALING WITH DESPAIR

1. Jonathan Schell, *The Fate of the Earth* (New York: Knopf, 1982).

Part II Nulcear Realities

NUCLEAR POWER

1. Anna Gyorgy and friends, *No Nukes* (Boston: South End Press, 1979), p. 112.
2. James Dodson, Ohio Edison nuclear spokesman, March 29, 1979 quoted in *The Real Paper*, Boston, April 21, 1979.
3. Dr. Helen Caldicott, *Genetic and Health Concerns*.

4. Dr. John Cobb, scientist, *New York Times*, February 5, 1979.

5. These findings have been summarized in many sources including *No Nukes*, cited above.

6. Robert Leppzer, *Voices from Three Mile Island: The People Speak Out* (Trumansburg, NY: The Crossing Press, 1980).

7. *U.S. News and World Report*, May 14, 1979.

8. *The Boston Globe*, November 4, 1981.

9. *Washington Post*, April 6, 1979.

10. Jimmy Breslin, "Scared Kids," *The Boston Globe*, April 6, 1979.

11. Leslie J. Freeman, *Nuclear Witnesses: Insiders Speak Out* (New York: W.W. Norton and Company, 1982), p. 44.

12. *Arizona Republic*, July 6, 1982.

13. Dr. Earnest Sternglass, "Three Mile Island Fallout," *The Boston Globe*, March 23, 1980.

14. Jane Lee, a farmer living two and a half miles from Three Mile Island, was quoted in a discussion with Greenpeace.

15. Nuclear Information Resource Service, "Nuclear Costs," Energy Fact Sheet No. 3, 1982. (NIRS, 1536 Sixteenth St. N.W., Washington, D.C. 20002).

16. *The Boston Globe*, April 18, 1979.

17. "Failure to Adequately Protect the American People from the Hazards of Radiation," Government Accounting Office Report, 1977.

18. For example, "a federal grand jury accused Metropolitan Edison Co. of deliberately falsifying key safety records and violating operating procedures in the months leading up to the March 1979 accident at its Three Mile Island Unit 2 reactor." (*The Philadelphia Inquirer*, November 8, 1983).

19. Department of Energy Fiscal Year Report 1984.

20. *Los Angeles Times*, May 7, 1982. "The Energy Department's Energy Information Administration said the final construction costs for 77 percent of the plants now operating were at least double the pre-construction estimates." (*The Philadelphia Inquirer*, January 18, 1984).

21. *Arizona Republic*, August 19, 1982.

NUCLEAR WEAPONS

1. *Washington Peace Center Newsletter*, November, 1981.

2. *The Real Paper*, November 27, 1980.

3. Dr. Earnest Sternglass, "Three Mile Island Fallout," *The Boston Globe*, March 23, 1980.

4. *The Boston Globe*, December 8, 1982.

5. The most frightening recent development is the contemplation and production of first-strike nuclear weapons. The decision by the United States and its NATO allies to employ 108 Pershing II Medium Range Ballistic Missiles and 465 Ground-Launched Cruise Missiles in Europe as well as the development and production of MX and other counterforce weapons means that the United States could potentially play an offensive role, reducing the effects of Soviet retaliation by intercepting enemy missiles that survive an initial U.S. assault. This potential situation undermines deterrence and makes each side more willing to launch its own attack before the enemy does. (Barbara Spratt, "First Strike Weapons," *Chain Reactions*, Volume 1, Issue 5, July 1983.)

6. Stacey Sweeney, aged fourteen, quoted by David Arnold, "The Young and Nuclear War: How Exactly Do They Feel?", *The Boston Globe*, October 29, 1981.

7. Frank Brodhead, "The Peace Movement Today," *The Mobilizer*, Vol. 2, No. 2, May, 1982.

8. All quotations in the margin of the "I Hate War" section are excerpts from the writing of children in third, sixth, seventh, tenth, eleventh and twelfth grade classes in Sacramento, California quoted in Norma R. Law, *Children and War* (Washington DC: Association for Childhood Education International, 1973).

Part III Alternatives

CHANGING OUR LIFE STYLES

1. Nancy Jack Todd, *The Village as Solar Ecology: Procedings of the New Alchemy/Generic Design Conference, April 16-21, 1979*, p. 7.

Part IV Taking Action For the World We Want

TAKING ACTION TOWARDS PEACE

1. Otto Nathan and Heinz Norden, eds., *Einstein on Peace* (New York: Schocken Books, 1968), p. 427.
2. More information is available from: The Cambridge Commission on Peace Education and Nuclear Disarmament, 57 Inman St., Cambridge, MA 02139.
3. Quoted in *Resist Newsletter*, December, 1981.
4. Complete copies of this statement are available from: Women's Pentagon Action, 339 Lafayette St., New York, NY 10012.
5. *New York Times*, November 12, 1983.

Afterword

by Dr. Helen Caldicott

Watermelons Not War" reiterates the need for every parent to face the nuclear weapons dilemma. But we don't have much time. The children know it. Some of them have spoken through the pages of this book about the haunting fear that they have no future. For the little ones, the monster in their closet may be a nuclear bomb; as they get older and begin to absorb the news from the TV and newspapers, and get a glimpse at how politicians and generals and corporate executives behave, they begin to question whether they will grow up at all, or whether their lives will be cut short by global catastrophe. They are becoming a generation of fatalists.

This doesn't have to be so. As adults who understand the stakes involved, and who live in a democratic society where individuals can have great power if they learn how to use it, we can provide another model for these children; a model that offers life instead of death; a model that calls for active participation in national decision making rather than passive acceptance of more and more powerful weapons; a model that shows our children a way out of their fatalism and a way into social responsibility.

We can still prevent the development of a defeatist attitude in our children. We have to prevent it. What it will take is a willingness to show our children what kind of stuff we are made of, and a determination to use our power as individuals in a democracy for everything it is worth. Nothing else matters.

Women's Action for Nuclear Disarmament
Boston, Massachusetts 1983

Resources

Books

Here is a list of currently available resources we have used and recommend. The books are divided into sections—

The Heart of the Matter
Human Reactions
Nuclear Power
Nuclear War
The Situation We Face
Alternatives
Peace
Possibilities and Visions

If you don't find a book on the shelves, most bookstores will be glad to order it. Libraries and school departments will often do the same.

Each section includes books for adults and children. The children's books were chosen to be a pleasure for people of all ages; they are arranged with the simplest ones at the beginning.

A list of organizations working on the issues we cover is also included.

The Heart of the Matter

For Adults

Tree of Life
   1981; available from UNICEF, 866 UN Plaza, New York, NY 10017
The World through the Eyes of Children— In 1969, a Swedish teacher asked her class to draw their visions of the Tree of Life. They reacted so enthusiastically that the idea spread. The 250 paintings and letters in this book, by children 8 to 12, from 80 countries, provide a way for people to find out directly from children what frightens them, what's important to them, what they love.

Children of Hiroshima
   compiled by Dr. Arato Osada; 1982 (Japanese original, 1960);
   Harper Colophon Books, New York
Eventually, a few doctors and teachers found the strength to study and interview the children of Hiroshima. What they found is deeply moving, sometimes astonishing. The President of Hiroshima University published 105 of these stories, arranged by age group, because he believed it is important for us to understand what they thought and felt.

Children as Teachers of Peace
   by our children, ed. by Gerald G. Jampolsky, MD; 1982; Celestial
   Arts., Millbrae, CA
What does peace mean to you? What is your experience of peace? 137 pictures, statements and letters were chosen from children's responses around the U.S. to the following topics:
   "Peace is _____"
   "What Peace Means to Me"
   "If I were a teacher to the world's leaders, what I would say to them to help bring peace is _____."

Their thoughts and advice are delightful, touching, and often profound.

Children and War
   Norma R. Law; 1973; available from Association for Childhood
   Education International, 3615 Wisconsin Ave., NW, Washington,
   D.C. 20016—35ᶜ each, 10 for $3.00
This pamphlet is the best short discussion we've found on what children
know about peace and war, how this knowledge affects them, and
what adults can do.

Parenting

Of course, the possibilities of total annihilation created by the continuing
growth of weapons systems increase the pressure. Around the country,
adults are acknowledging—and reacting to— the effects of the nuclear
age on children. These two excellent and useful booklets were written
by groups formed out of parents' concern, and their determination to
protect their children.

What Shall We Tell the Children?
   by Parenting in the Nuclear Age; 1983; 22 pages—available from 6501
   Telegraph Ave., Oakland, CA 94609
This booklet contains chapters on:

   —Confronting Our Own Despair
   —Talking with Kids (in sections for different ages)
   —Things for Kids to Do
   —Gaining Strength from Each Other
   —Frequent Questions and Answers
   —Finding Consolation and Renewal

It is filled with delightful illustrations.

What About the Children?
   by Parents and Teachers for Social Responsibility; 1983; 15 pages—
   available from PTSR, Box 517, Moretown, VT 05660 (Please include
   a donation to cover printing and mailing costs.)
The authors believe that asking this question in all circumstances is in itself,
a significant way to begin making the many changes that must be
undertaken. A short review of the interwoven threats we are all being
exposed to is followed by long lists of little actions—"small flags"—to choose
from.

Parenting for Peace and Justice
   Kathleen and James McGinnis; 1981; Orbis Books, Maryknoll, NY
Rather than focusing on separate problems and situations, as most child-
care books do, the McGinnis' share information and ideas they've gathered
from other families and their own efforts to include children in life. Through
examples, they discuss how questions of peace, violence, faith, culture and
role actually appear on a daily basis, and demonstrate what can be done
to raise children with due regard for material necessities, self-initiative, and
human dignity. Writing from a deep Christian orientation, they describe
the obstacles as well as the options, taking as their motto, "One step at
a time."

ed. by Ronnie Friedland and Carol Kort; 1981; Houghton Mifflin, Boston
Shared Experiences—74 first-hand accounts by mothers in different situations, who discuss events from pregnancy to death. They speak openly of their feelings; of changing relationships with children, husbands, family, friends, and with themselves. In sharing experiences of great personal importance, they give us insights into how we are affected by both the unexpected and unacknowledged jolts of ordinary life, and how we react to its surprises. The last piece, "Despair, Hope and Motherhood," was written by an NEP member.

For Children

The Fall of Freddy the Leaf
Leo Buscaglia; 1982; Charles B. Slack, Inc., Thorofare, NJ
A Story of Life for All Ages—Beautiful photographs follow Freddy and his companions from winter bud to autumn color and fall. The words give his conversations with a special friend: 'Why is each leaf of the same tree different?'—'Why do we change?'—'What's down there?'—and point out that it's not possible to photograph Freddy after his form is redissolved into the world.

Goodnight, Dear Monster
Terry Nell Morris; 1980; Knopf, New York
It's bedtime, and you're sleepy, so what do you do when a monster comes out and scares your stuffed animal? Well, you can get angry and scare the monster right back. That's when things get really interesting. We've heard grownups laugh out loud as they read this book without words.

Elephant on Wheels
Alida McKay Thacher; 1974; Western Publishing, Racine, WI
Petunia likes to roller skate. Her family says, "Elephants don't skate." Petunia answers their objections, but what will she do when they get together and plan to hide the skates? Suspense and a surprise twist at the end. An Eager Reader Little Golden Book.

The Cat Who Stamped His Feet
Betty R. Wright; 1974; Western Publishing, Racine, WI
Clancy withdraws in a rage when his family brings a stranger into his orderly and comfortable life without consulting him. Although bored by himself, it takes a request for help and information from the new cat to start Clancy looking at how the arrangement really does affect him. Another Eager Reader.

Dorrie and the Dreamyard Monsters
Patricia Coombs; 1982; Dell Pub., New York
Dorrie is a witch. "A little witch. Her hat is always on crooked and her socks never match." All over Witchville, dreams are turning into nightmares. An attempt is made to send the Dream Witch more of

the potion used to control the monsters who've taken over. (They're pink and furry.) If the plan had worked as planned, it would have failed. But one mix-up after another, plus Dorrie's quick wits, produce a better solution.

Charlotte's Web
E.B. White; 1952; Harper & Row, New York
Life in the Zuckerman's barnyard is beginning to seem lonely and boring to young Wilbur the pig, until a special friendship develops between him and Charlotte. When the old sheep tells them that Wilbur is headed for bacon, Charlotte draws on her patience, versatility and knowledge of human nature ("People believe almost anything they see in print.") to save him. But they both need the help of Templeton the rat ("You know how he is—always looking out for himself, never thinking of the other fellow.")

The Secret Garden
Frances Hodgson Burnett; 1971; Dell Publishing Co., New York
Mary is an obstinate, sour little girl, who's been given every luxury money can buy, and not much else. Her ambition to revive an abandoned garden involves two boys: Dickon, who knows wild things so well he can talk to robins; and Colin, a spoiled and frightened invalid. During a long spring and summer, they fight, play, and thrive, as the joyful months and the adventure of growing fill them with a sense of magic.

Taran Wanderer
Lloyd Alexander; 1969; Dell Publishing Co., New York
Taran, Assistant Pig-Keeper, sets out through the land of Prydain, seeking to become a hero, and noble enough to marry the tomboy princess he loves. He fails to achieve the goals he'd dreamed of, but through encounters he could never have imagined or predicted, grows up, and finds himself.

For Adults

Despair and Personal Power in the Nuclear Age
   Joanna Macy; 1983; New Society Publishers, Philadelphia
It is often hard to acknowledge our reactions, and harder yet to feel them. The activities described in this thoughtful book make it possible to experience then *use* the power of these feelings. There is a short, but excellent section on children's needs, and ways to respond to them.

Psychosocial Aspects of Nuclear Developments
   William Beardslee, M.D. and John Mack, M.D.; 1982; American
   Psychiatric Association Task Force Report #20—available from APA
   Publications, Washington, DC
As doctors have begun to investigate and publicize the physical effects of nuclear technology and destruction, mental health experts are looking at the psychological effects. Their work experience in dealing with the dangerous consequences of denial, and the ideas and skills that enable people to confront difficulties successfully, are applied in seven areas: the arms race, Soviet-American relationships, secrecy, Three-Mile Island, reactions to nuclear power in other countries, adult responses, and the impact on children and adolescents. In their conclusion, the authors say that because of the fear and pain involved, it was only "in working together through shared concern that we have found that we have been able to work at all."

The 100th Monkey
   Ken Keyes, Jr.; 1982; Vision Books, St. Mary, KY 40063
Inspired by the Hundredth Monkey Phenomenon, described in "The Heart of the Matter", and by a film, "The Final Epidemic", Keyes has compiled a short picture of the nuclear monster, from megatons to millirems; examples of the power of newly emerging priorities; and how to change our actions and mental habits from the myth of 'me vs. you' to the reality of 'we're all in this together'.

The Plague
   Albert Camus; 1972; Random House, New York
Wandering through a city that is quarantined and totally isolated finally by an epidemic of bubonic plague, a disease for which there is no cure, a doctor observes the different ways he and the other inhabitants react to the presence of death, the possibility of dying, and the disruption of normal existence. The classic novel of modern times.

The Color Purple
   Alice Walker; 1982; Harcourt Brace Jovanovich, New York
"You better not never tell nobody but God. It'd kill your mammy." So Celie writes letters to God. Along with the letters from and to her beloved sister, Nettie, faraway, they reveal more than thirty years of the rich tapestry of people's lives. As Shug says, "I think it pisses God off if you walk by the color purple in a field somewhere and don't

notice it." What everybody *does* see, how they sustain themselves, what they achieve and how they change—the bonds of blood, spirit and love between women—all this comes to the reader with pain, honesty, and humor. This novel won the Pulitzer Prize.

Cat's Cradle
Kurt Vonnegut, Jr.; 1974; Dell Publishing Co., New York
Cynical, sad, and funny, this satire recounts the doings and foibles of a varied group of characters linked by a self-centered scientist's creation—a form of water that freezes at room temperature. A book that cries 'What's the use?' with an angry laugh of despair.

M.A.S.H.
Richard Hooker; 1975; Pocket Books, New York
Assign people trained to save lives to the job of patching up soldiers who will be sent back to the front if they recover. Alternate long periods of too much work with none at all. Individually and collectively, the personnel of M.A.S.H. react to an absurd situation by getting the job done, and creating some absurdity of their own. The TV series was based on this wild and wacky story.

The Nuclear Family Vacation Guide
Shepherd/Woods/Kay; 1982; available from 36 Webster Rd., Milton, MA 02186
Making the Most of a Nuclear Attack on Your City—Real laughter *is* a great medicine. And it's available in this tongue-in-cheek collection of handy hints and illustrations. After all, "One unique aspect of your Nuclear Holiday is that you will never have to tell your children that the party's over, and that everyone has to go home. Since there will be no home to go to, you'll be able to make yourselves a brand new home, in a brand new world, *your* world."

For Children

The Snowy Day
Ezra Jack Keats; 1962; Viking Press, New York
In the kind of experience that's common for young children, a little boy explores the delights of a world that's miraculously changed. In plain words and pictures of great beauty, Keats communicates the depth and feeling of simple events.

One Morning in Maine
Robert McCloskey; 1953; Viking Press, New York
On the morning Sal gets up, walks down the beach to work with her father, loses her first tooth, and goes to the store, it seems that she notices growth, loss, and change all around her . . . "And there's clam chowder for lunch!"

The Little Prince
Antoine De Saint Exupery; 1943; Harcourt Brace Jovanovich, New York

The pilot of a plane forced down in the desert with engine trouble is astonished when a little boy appears, and asks him to draw a sheep. The boy has left his own small planet because he doesn't know how to get along with a demanding friend. The adults he's met in his travels have made mixed-up choices themselves, but a fox has taught him that the significance of a thing comes from the meaning it has for you—and to find that meaning, it's best to search with the heart. Knowing that he loves his friend, he's come back to his departure point in the desert, and from there returns home.

Bridge to Teribithia
Katherine Paterson; 1979; Avon Books, New York

Jess plans to make it through the fifth grade by practicing enough to be the best sprinter in his class. But he really hits it off with the new kid who's moved in down the road. Her style is so different from the local norm that school gets more difficult, while the rest of the day becomes an adventure, as they make a private Kingdom of their own. But a sad time comes, when sharing that special world of enchantment is the only way to carry it on.

The Day No Pigs Would Die
Robert N. Peck; 1972; Knopf, New York

"Being his son was like knowing a king." In a moving and funny novel based on the author's own boyhood and family, the reader comes to understand and share this deep feeling for the poor farmer whose integrity, commitment and humor inspire such love. The characters need the strength they get from the warmth, laughter and rewards of a homely outlook on life that "goes back to earthy reason." Sometimes the reason is hard.

Where the Sidewalk Ends
Shel Silverstein; 1974; Harper & Row, New York

We learn to hide thoughts that feel unusual, scary, or unacceptable. Silverstein has pulled out a good selection, and turned them into jokes and poetry that children love. For example: "Spaghetti, spaghetti, all over the place, Up to my elbows—up to my face, Over the carpet and under the chairs . . . "

Nuclear Power   *For Adults*

No Nukes
Anna Gyorgy and Friends; 1979; South End Press, Boston
Everyone's Guide to Nuclear Power—The basic book for learning about nuclear power (and alternatives), *No Nukes* gives clear, complete explanations of every phase in the production of nuclear power, and the dangers to environmental and human health posed by each one. The many simple diagrams and illustrations make scientific questions—'What's a nucleus?' 'What does radiation do to you?'—easy to understand.

Energy Future
ed. by Robert Stobaugh and Daniel Yergin; 1982; Random House, New York
The result of a 6-year study at the Harvard Business School, this report is divided into chapters examining oil, gas, nuclear power, and solar alternatives. Surprisingly, the researchers discovered that *conservation* is the most important energy source available if we want to preserve our 'American lifestyle'.

Voices from Three Mile Island
Robert Leppzer; 1980; Crossing Press, Trumansburg, NY
The People Speak Out—An opportunity to hear the inside story of the effects of a nuclear accident from the engineers, residents, workers, parents, farmers, etc., who have lived through one.

Grass Roots
ed. by Fred Wilcox; 1980; Crossing Press, Trumansburg, NY
An Anti-Nuke Sourcebook—"But what can we do?" Lots. *Grass Roots* gives examples of what and how. Experienced people from all over the country explain how to form an organization, start a petition, detect low-level radiation, monitor your local utility, pass a transportation ban, and much more. Each section has a list of materials and organizations that can be helpful.

Nuclear Power for Beginners
Stephen Croall and Kai Anders; 1978; Pantheon, New York
The history of nuclear power, facts and figures on its effects (cancer, clean-up requirements, lost jobs, etc.) and the threats it poses to our political and economic system are described in a lively comic book format. The possibilities of 'soft energy' are covered, and the book ends with lists of anti-nuclear organizations, books, and films. Teachers find that many teenagers enjoy its zip and humor.

The Legend of King Midas
  available in many storybooks
How do you explain to a child the powerful and far reaching effects of something like radiation, that no one can even see? The old story of the king who gets his wish to change anything he touches into gold can help. (Not only does this power ruin his food and drink, but when his child hugs him, she turns into gold too! Luckily, the gods return everything to normal.)

Serendipity
  Stephen Congreve; 1974; Serendipity Press, Bothell, WA
A lonely young sea monster finds that having friends and something she feels is important to do (returning the garbage people throw in the water to the dumpers) make for an enjoyable and interesting life.

The Stonecutter
  Gerald McDermott; 1975; Penguin Books, New York
Have you ever dreamed of being so powerful that you can do anything you want, and not be affected by anyone or anything? A young man who has the help of a spirit in achieving this state finds himself in an unexpected spot.

Bartholemew and the Oobleck
  Dr. Seuss; 1949; Random House, New York
King Derwin feels something new should fall from the sky—not just your old-fashioned rain, sleet or snow. His magicians think it's an interesting problem—and they succeed in solving it. After a lot of consultations and panting and puffing, Bartholomew gets the mess stopped and the cleanup organized.

Mistress Masham's Repose
  T.H. White; 1979; Berkeley Publishing Co., San Francisco
A 10-year old wants to help a "lost colony" of Lilliputians. The power of might is contrasted with the power of community, as she discovers that being bigger and stronger doesn't mean that she can solve their problems. Whimsical, and very funny.

Zeely
  Virginia Hamilton; 1967; MacMillan, New York
In many fairy tales, goose girls and swineherds turn out to be queens and kings. Dreams lure Elizabeth to ignore the friends and pleasures of a special summer, until Zeely shows her that dreams give us most when they deepen our understanding of real life.

Nuclear Weapons

For Adults

The Fate of the Earth
Jonathan Schell; 1982; Knopf, New York

Although we have lived with the facts for a while, it's difficult to focus on the consequences of nuclear war. For over 15 years, Mr. Schell committed himself to this duty, and shares the knowledge with a tenderness and love that makes it possible " . . . to awaken to the truth of our peril, a truth as great as life itself . . . "

Unforgettable Fire
ed. by Japanese Broadcasting Corp,; 1977; Pantheon Books, New York

When an old man visited Channel NHK with a drawing he wanted to leave to posterity, the TV station sent out a request for pictures from other survivors of the Hiroshima A-Bomb. This simple collection of 104 of those drawings and paintings is the closest we can come to the knowledge of nuclear war without experiencing it ourselves.

Nuclear War: What's In It for You?
Ground Zero; 1982; Pocket Books, New York

A very readable basic book that explains how nuclear war might start, what the results would be, and actions that will help to prevent it. Ground Zero was formed as a strictly non-partisan, non-advocacy educational organization, "dedicated to supplying information that the public has a right to know."

What About the Russians—and Nuclear War?
Ground Zero; 1983; Pocket Books, New York

"The policies of the Soviet Union, whether we like them or not, are fundamental when we think about American security." In this book, Ground Zero has collected information from over 60 professional Soviet observers and national security experts on:

—Russian and Soviet history
—their economy, character and everyday life
—the workings of the Soviet political system
—foreign policy and actions since World War II
—the Soviet military challenge
—the future of Soviet-U.S. relations

"Is This Blue Marble Big Enough for the Both of Us?"

The Threat
Andrew Cockburn; 1983; Random House, New York

Inside the Soviet Military Machine—The Soviets, with a population of ethnic groups even more diverse than ours (only half are 'Russians'), a harsher climate, and a long history of tensions with surrounding countries, put even more of their resources into the military system than we do. What do they get for this investment? Using first-hand sources, Cockburn surveys the equipment, weapons and supply systems, as well as the bureaucracy, personnel and politics of their armed forces, to give the general reader a real look at the "true shape and scope of Soviet military capability."

Gyn/Ecology
Mary Daly; 1978; Beacon Press, Boston
The Metaethics of Radical Feminism—This remarkable, though difficult, book examines the many ways violence and cruelty are embedded in American and European cultures, and expressed in our governments, churches, schools and other institutions. It explains how our fears of self-acceptance and revenge tempt us to act against our common sense.

Slaughterhouse 5
Kurt Vonnegut, Jr.; 1974; Dell Publishing Co., New York
Or the Children's Crusade— On August 6, more than 71,000 people died in the A-bomb attack on Hiroshima. In Tokyo on March 9, over 83,000 people, and in Dresden on February 13, over 135,000 were killed by 'conventional' bombs. The few who survived the fire-storm of Dresden emerged from their shelters into a world they could see, but not imagine. Twenty-five years later, an American novelist who was a P.O.W. there, gave up trying to make sense of it and included his experiences in a comic patchwork of fantasy, war, and suburbia.

On the Beach
Nevil Shute; 1978; Ballantine, New York
First published in 1957, this best-selling, quiet story has given many readers their first glimpse of a nuclear future. The crew of an American submarine surfaces in the South Pacific to the realization that a nuclear war has been fought. We follow them and the Australians they meet, work with, and love while experts track the radioactive cloud spreading south.

Jenny
Yorick Blumenfeld; 1982; Little, Brown & Co., Boston
Jenny, her husband, and selected friends have made preparations to survive the coming nuclear holocaust. Written in diary form, this novel takes place during the following years in their well designed, fortified and stocked shelter. Fascinating, but not fun to read.

For Children

Island of the Skog
Stephen Kellogg; 1976; Dial Press, New York
Trouble with a cat is making life in the neighborhood store too difficult, so an adventurous group of mice set off to sea in true pioneering fashion. When they discover that the island they've moved to is already inhabited, they think they must prepare for war. But . . .

The Tomato Patch

William Wondriska; 1964; Holt, Rinehart & Winston, New York
Two princes, and eventually two countries, conclude that maintaining a state of war just doesn't have the appeal of a ripe tomato.

How the Children Stopped Wars

Jan Wahl; 1969; Avon Books, New York
A boy sets out to find his father, who is fighting in the war. Other children come along to find *their* fathers. It is a long and difficult journey, but they persist, and find their way to where the soldiers are fighting. Fathers, uncles and brothers are found. And then . . . Mr. Wahl was inspired by the feeling that today's children need new fairy tales.

The Pushcart War

Jean Merril; 1964; Dell Publishing Co., New York
An absolutely delightful introduction to all the steps of a 'traditional' war, including outbreak of hostilities, escalation, strategies, sabotage, surrender, peace conferences, and the movie epic made on location.

Sadako and the Thousand Paper Cranes

Eleanor Coerr; 1977; G.P. Putnam & Sons, New York
Exposed to radiation in Hiroshima, 11-year old Sadako develops leukemia in 1954. In the hospital, she begins to fold paper cranes, following the tradition that the person who folds 1000 will be restored to health. She dies before they are done, but other children continue for her. Teachers use this true story because it enables children to learn the facts and grieve along with the girls and boys in the book. It ends with the simple directions for making paper cranes.

My Enemy, My Brother

James Forman; 1972; Scholastic Book Services, New York
A group of Jewish teenagers leave the concentration camps and war-ravaged lands of Europe for Israel. In their own ways, each one meets the demands of new surroundings, peace and adult life. But war is declared and they must fight their Palestinian and Bedouin neighbors. This book makes few judgments, and offers no answers. In many ways, it explains the realities of problems in the Middle East better than current news reports.

The Diary of Anne Frank

1979; Pendulum Press, West Haven, CT
Anne Frank was one of seven, then eight, Dutch Jews who were hidden in the attic rooms of an office building for two years. Her diary contains the normal concerns and interest of a teenager—family life, boys, privacy, her future, the faults of grownups. Children respond to a voice their own age; for adults, it's encouraging to read of the spirit and vitality with which she lived, despite the restricted and dangerous circumstances.

For Adults

Nuclear Madness—What You Can Do
Helen Caldicott, M.D.; 1978; Autumn Press, Brookline, MA
A simple and passionate introduction to the topic, with short, clear explanations of the nuclear fuel cycle, the effects on our health of nuclear radiation and plutonium,and the dangers to us in current defense and weapons strategies. It begins with a step-by-step description of how, in 1971, growing public reaction to her information on the dangers of nuclear testing led Australia and New Zealand to bring France before the International Court of Justice in 1973, and France to stop the explosions in 1974.

Indefensible Weapons
Robert J. Lifton and Richard Falk; 1982; Basic Books, New York. In this clear and deeply felt work, a psychiatrist and an international lawyer explore the political, psychological, and military problems created by our dependence on nuclear weapons. This book helps us think about our complicity and its effects on ourselves and our children. It helps us consider possible ways of extricating ourselves from the nuclear age.

Nuclear Witnesses: Insiders Speak Out
Leslie J. Freeman; 1981; W.W. Norton & Co., New York
Feeling that the truth was a matter of life and death when a doctor prescribed radioactive iodine, Mr. Freeman went directly to those who work in nuclear technology for information. This book is a compilation of the actual words of a worker in a nuclear power plant, a researcher on low-level radiation, a weapons physicist, a director of a government bio-medical research laboratory, a nuclear power plant construction worker, a uranium miner, the widows of two uranium miners, a Navajo organizer, an atomic military veteran, a reprocessing plant supervisor, and four safety inspectors and engineers.

Hillbilly Women
Kathy Kahn; 1972; Avon Books, New York
Many —most— people in the world today live in hard times. How do they get along? In this collection we get to hear 19 ordinary, and yet remarkable, real-life stories. The strength, pride, humor, and the values of religion, music and kin which have sustained these women shine in their words. From their experiences (and her own), the editor concludes that it takes anger to make changes.

The Silent Intruder
Charles Panati and Michel Hudson; 1981; Houghton Mifflin, Boston
Surivivng the Radiation Age— Essential reading for anyone who cares about how we and our children are being affected by radiation *right now*. This book is especially important because it describes *all* the forms of radiation to which we are being exposed: X-rays; nature's own radiation; 'electric smog' from radio, TV, radar, microwave, high-

power lines, etc.; radioactive garbage; and the current impact of nuclear power and bomb production. For each of these sources, personal, local and national steps we can take to protect ourselves are covered.

Killing Our Own

Harvey Wasserman et al; 1982; Dell Publishing Co., New York
The Disaster of America's Experience with Atomic Radiation—An up-to-date history of nuclear technology, giving us a sobering look at the generally unpublicized risks to which we are being exposed. The authors are reporters, and their investigations take us into the corridors and backrooms of hospitals, laboratories, government and the courts, as they follow people who are trying to get answers instead of false reassurances about what's going on. The book begins with an excellent map: 'Atomic Radation in America', and ends with Appendices on: 1) The basics of radiation and health, 2) A summary of atomic bomb testing, 3) Commercial nuclear power reactors in the U.S., and 4) Organizations to contact or join.

At Highest Risk

Christopher Norwood; 1980; McGraw Hill, New York
Environmental Hazards to Young and Unborn Children— The pre-born, infants, and children are more affected by radiation and pollution than older people. This book details the dangers, and gives some ideas about how we can protect our children.

Of Woman Born

Adrienne Rich; 1976; Bantam Books, New York
There are facts: all people grow in a woman's body, and when born must be cared for by others in order to survive; we move and feel; we all die. There are institutions which express their requirements through the concepts, definitions, ideals, stereotypes and roles they apply to such facts; and which give us the responsibility of carrying out the 'rules' without the power to affect what the 'rules' are. In a profound, angry and tender investigation of motherhood, Rich explores the effects of this crucial distinction. She asks that we use the unacknowledged potential of our "thinking bodies" to create the visions and terms of our lives.

Disturbing the Universe

Freeman Dyson; 1981; Harper & Row, New York
A Life in Science—Reading this memoir can give the feeling of being personally acquainted with a scientist from childhood on. Dyson introduces us to his family, friends and fellow workers, describes the circumstances that led him—a theoretical physicist and political pacifist—to designing atomic bombs, then tells us what he's been doing since.

A People's History of the United States

Howard Zinn; 1981; Harper & Row, New York
Standard history books describe events that involved the men in power. Professor Zinn concentrates on the hidden history of the other 99%.

From the arrival of Columbus to the end of the 1970s, he follows ordinary people; he describes what their lives were like, how laws, policies and social movements affected them, the parts they played in the events of their times. Fascinating, and a real eye-opener.

The State of the World Atlas
Michael Kidson and Alan Segal; 1982; Simon & Schuster, New York
63 maps of the world have been colored so you can see and compare statistics for yourself. For example: who has, makes, sells and buys nuclear weapons; which countries have nuclear power plants; infant mortality rates throughout the world.

Consider the Process of Living
William H. Eddy, Jr., Gonzalo Leon and Robert Milne; 1972; the Conservation Foundation, Washington, DC
"The increasing demands of a growing human population, coupled with the power of man's technology, have changed our planet's face. Some of this change has brought great benefits. But some of it, too, now threatens the very process of living." So that we can understand these threats, and their importance to us, this splendid book uses beautiful pictures, color photographs, and simple words to explain the air, water, earth, energy, and life of our world: what they are, how they come to be, and how changes in one affect the rest.

Why do we include references to TV, and to commercial programs in the schools? In examining our situation as parents, experience with our own children and the studies we've seen have indicated that most of children's information and conclusions about the larger world come from these sources. To know their situation, we must know how they are affected by the vast resources directed at them.

Influencing Children

The ACT Guide to Children's Television
Evelyn Kay; 1979; Beacon Press, Boston
How to Treat TV with TLC—The emphasis is on teaching children to understand and use TV instead of being used by it. Both ways to reduce the effects of the violence, prejudice, greed and confusion children are exposed to, and creative uses of TV are covered. "A Children's Workbook" helps children over eight to:

—investigate their own viewing habits
—compare TV watching to other activities they enjoy
—develop a more objective reaction to commercials and programs.

There are rating charts, experiments, and guides to making their own ads, cartoons and programs. The final section, "What You Can Do", is based on the success that ACT, a grassroots organization, has had during the last fourteen years in helping broadcasters, regulatory agencies and program sponsors meet their responsibilities to children and to the public.

The Plug-In Drug
Marie Winn; 1977; Viking Press, New York

Winn focuses on what is really happening when children watch TV. The main point is that they *are* watching TV, instead of doing other things; in effect shortening their childhood by five to seven hours a day, on the average. The reasons parents encourage or accept TV-watching are thoroughly and sensitively discussed, and many solutions that have worked for other parents are described.

Four Arguments for the Elimination of Television
Jerry Mander; 1978; William Morrow & Co., New York

It's not natural to stare at a small lit-up surface for hours. Our emotional, mental, physical and social health—our whole country's well-being—is more affected than we realize. This long, but gripping, study surveys what is currently known about the loss of power and control, the isolation and deprivation produced by TV technology.

Hucksters in the Classroom
Sheila Harty; 1979; Center for the Study of Responsive Law, Washington, DC

A Review of Industry Propaganda in Schools—The harsh facts that:

—American schools spend about one percent of their budgets on books and other educational materials
—It's good business sense for 'educators' employed by corporations to gain access to students with beautifully designed 'free' books, films, lectures, field trips, etc.

The first section of this thorough and readable study examines the effects of these commercial 'offerings', which most children in our schools are being exposed to right now. It covers the four areas where most are currently concentrated: food, energy, environment and economics. The second section describes efforts at evaluation and review of such materials, and possible initiatives for improvement. Actual illustrations from the material appear on almost every page.

The Family of Man
Edward Steichen; 1955; Museum of Modern Art, New York
People at work and play; during the significant moments of life; in joy, anger, grief—or simply being; in conflict and comradeship; alone and together. Children and grownups turn the pages of this classic collection of 503 photographs from around the world again and again, always finding something that strikes the heart.

People
Peter Spier; 1980; Doubleday & Co., New York
This magnificent picture book also gives children the rare chance to look at lots and lots of different people: wearing different clothes, living, working, and enjoying themselves in different ways. For contrast to that richness and variety, it ends with a scene in which everybody looks just the same.

Cloudy With a Chance of Meatballs
Judi Barret; 1981; Atheneum, New York
Once upon a time the weather report predicted the food supply. Everyone took it for granted that their system was great, so when changes come, the action gets pretty hectic.

Julie of the Wolves
Jean C. George; 1972; Harper & Row, New York
Driven by circumstance to try crossing the Canadian Arctic alone, a young Eskimo girl is assisted, and then befriended by a pack of wolves. As she gets to know them and their life, so do we.

Alice in Wonderland
Lewis Carrol; many editions available
As children do, Alice manages to enjoy herself, even in a topsy-turvy world where she's always getting bigger or smaller, and characters including the Queen of Hearts and the Mad Hatter play croquet using flamingos for mallets.

Through the Looking Glass
Lewis Carrol; many editions available
This time Alice walks through a mirror into a land where everything is backwards, and where you have to keep running to stay in the same place. Humpty Dumpty, Tweedle Dum and Tweedle Dee contribute to the nonsense.

A Wrinkle in Time
Madeline L'Engle; 1962; Dell Publishing Co., New York
Their father has gone on a dangerous mission and has not returned. When the Murray children and their friend Calvin O'Keefe go looking for him, they discover that some 'reasonable' things are scary, and that some 'weird' things are comfortable.

A Wind in the Door

Madeline L'Engle; 1973; Dell Publishing Co., New York

Charles Wallace Murray isn't getting along with the other children in school, and the cold, annoying principal doesn't help. But when his mother's scientific research shows something else is wrong with him too, it takes the principal's bravery, and understanding of the importance of small changes, to save Charles' life.

The Once and Future King

T.H. White; 1962; Dell Publishing Co., New York

A famous quartet of novels based on the legends of Camelot. King Arthur uses his skills and power to change the world, but human desires (his own included), interfere with his plans. Full of humor, mystery and warm understanding of the human condition; suitable for older teenagers.

Chains, Webs and Pyramids

Laurence Pringle; 1975; Thomas Crowell Co., New York

The Flow of Energy in Nature—The terms scientists use to investigate life systems are clearly diagrammed, illustrated and demonstrated by tracing examples through interwoven communities in two locations, a salt marsh and a field. Designed for grade-schoolers, it is an excellent introduction for anyone who wants to know how we are personally affected by food chains, predation pyramids, and changes in the interdependent webs of life.

For Adults

Soft Energy Paths
    Amory B. Lovins; 1977; Harper Colophon, New York
Toward a Durable Peace—How energy is made and used affects our lives in many ways. The different technologies available and the consequences of using them (including how much they cost us) are compared. Although the author, who is a physicist, considers and clearly explains the technical details, he believes that the choices we must make are basically political, social and ethical.

The Unsettling of America
    Wendell Berry; 1977; Avon Books, New York
Culture and Agriculture—Most of the food we eat nowadays comes not from farms, but from 'modern agribusiness'. How has this change affected our society? Berry, a poet, farmer and teacher, argues that the loss of the discipline, involvement, and love required by farming is impoverishing our culture and spirit.

We Didn't Have Much, but We Sure Had Plenty
    Sherry Thomas; Doubleday & Co., New York
In compiling these stories of rural women, Thomas discovered "ways of life fundamentally different" from what she had known. She feels that learning about their families, work, memories, and goals "enriches our sense of the possible." This book has the special excitement of meeting real people.

Muddling Toward Frugality
    Warren Johnson; 1978; Shambhala Publications, Boulder, CO
A Blueprint for Survival in the 1980s—The 'affluent society' is becoming less comfortable, less peaceful, less secure. "If the earth is to be a true home for us, a place of refuge and nurture, we may as well start to think about how we can make it such a place." For background, Johnson starts with a fascinating description of the main changes in the human life style since our beginnings. He shows why changes in our current system are always going on, and how we muddle through. If the pace of change is slow enough, he has confidence in the proven resilience and ability of the American democratic process and people to create new opportunities in new circumstances.

Woman and Nature
    Susan Griffin; 1978; Harper & Row, New York
The Roaring Inside Her—"Because we know ourselves to be made from this earth . . . as we speak to each other of what we know: the light is in us." The intense feminist vision of this poetic book can provide an experience, both spiritual and physical, of power as a transforming force.

The Way
   ed. by Shirley Hill Witt and Stan Steiner; 1972; Knopf, New York
One undeveloped resource we have is knowledge of how other cultures approach life. By finding out, we can expand our own understanding of what options are available. In the introduction to this anthology of writings from the many nations who lived on this continent before the European immigrations, the editors (an anthropologist and a writer) say, "You are soon to meet Indian thoughts as they were meant to be understood and have not been. You are to experience Indian logic as it naturally flows. You will witness the coalescence of America's ancient, original tradition with present-day language and problems."

Energy Primer
   ed. by Richard Merrill and Thomas Gage; 1978; Delta Books, New York
Solar, Water, Wind and Biofuels—For those who want to convert to renewable energy sources at home and/or on a local level, this readable and comprehensive introduction is a good place to start. It contains detailed descriptions of specific solutions; a catalogue of books, equipment and hardware; and engineering designs and specifications for actual energy sources. Sources range from alcohol stills and aquaculture ponds to windmills and wood-burning stoves. There are graphs, tables and hundreds of illustrations.

A Golden Thread
   Ken Butti and John Perkins; 1981; Cheshire Books, Palo Alto, CA
2500 Years of Solar Architecture and Technology—Much of the knowledge we need to save energy and be more comfortable has been in use around the world for centuries. Using clear and beautiful drawings, this book explains the principles involved and how they can be applied.

For Children

Three Strong Women
   Claus Stamm; 1962; Viking Press, New York
A Tall Tale from Japan—One of the kingdom's best wrestlers got so much better by studying with three women, that no one else can wrestle with him, and the sport is ruined when he competes. So, laden with glory and prize money, he returns to the country and becomes a farmer.

Many Moons
   James Thurber; 1943; Harcourt Brace Jovanovich, New York
The princess wants the moon; the king's advisers explain (in detail!) how impossible it is to get. Only the court jester knows that when you're helping someone, it's wise to start by finding out exactly what they're asking for.

Mike Mulligan and His Steam Shovel
   Virginia L. Burton; 1939; Houghton Mifflin, Boston
Although still good at their work, Mike and his steam shovel, Mary
Anne, have lost their place in the world they helped to build. Mike's
initiative in getting them a job, support from onlookers, and a little
boy's enthusiasm and good ideas produce a surprising and satisfying
new arrangement.

Understood Betsy
   Dorothy Canfield; 1981; Buccaneer Books, Cutchogue, NY
A young orphan in the early 1900s has her home in the city, where
she is protected, amused, and given "all the advantages" by a dedicated
and loving aunt. Because of illness in the family, she is sent to stay
with relatives on a poor farm, where she is given chores, sent to a
one-room schoolhouse, and expected to look out for herself. By the
time she is allowed to choose between the two homes, she has
discovered what matters most.

The Little House on the Prairie Series
   Laura Ingalls Wilder; Harper & Row, New York
Set on the American frontier, as it changes from Wisconsin to Nebraska
during the 1860s to 1880s, these memories of pioneer life, its hardships
and joys, are based on the author's own experiences. These are stories
with the flavor, uncertainty, and drama of real life.

Mrs. Frisby & the Rats of NIMH
   Robert C. O'Brien; 1971; Atheneum, New York
Mrs. Frisby's sick child will die if the family moves to escape the
farmer's plow. Although she sees no solution, she must try to find
one. "But where?" A crow she's helped takes her to the old owl, who
sends her to the rats of NIMH—rats who've been using their great
powers to make life so easy that it seems pointless. They have an
answer for Mrs. Frisby; but is there any answer for them?

Roll of Thunder, Hear My Cry
   Mildred Taylor; 1978; Bantam Books, New York
"I want these children to know we tried, and what we can't do now,
maybe one day they will." Sustained by the warmth and security that
comes from respect for their family, land and history, Cassie Logan
and her brothers learn to maintain their independence and humanity
in a community under pressure; and, if one way won't work, to look
for another.

The Children's Solar Energy Book even grownups can understand
   Tilly Spetgang and Malcolm Wells; 1982; Sterling Publishing Co.,
   New York
From "How It All Began" to "Solar Cells", the basic facts and 'how-
to's' of solar energy are covered in an amusing comic book format.
A good glossary, and energy experiments that can be done at home
are included.

Save the Earth
  Betty Miles; 1974; Knopf, New York
An Ecology Handbook for Kids—"Ecology is the study of the changes, and the connections on the earth." A beautifully designed handbook, full of simple, effective projects, and actions children can take that really make a difference. A great introduction to the subject for anyone, kids think it's terrific.

Peace

For Adults

Einstein on Peace
  ed. by Otto Nathan and Heinz Norden; 1968; Schocken Books, New York
Because he believed it is unreasonable for governments to settle disputes by killing people, and that the effects of military systems violate our dignity and freedom, Einstein was a committed pacifist. His letters and public statements, from the outbreak of World War I, in 1914, to the famous declaration warning of world death from nuclear weapons and urging governments to develop peaceful means of resolving their conflicts, which he signed a few days before his death in 1955, are collected in this book.

Education for Peace
  ed. by George Henderson; 1973; Association for Supervision and Curriculum Development, 225 N. Washington St., Alexandria, VA
Focus on Mankind—Eight short articles on the active development of peace cover:

  —Concepts of peace
  —Necessary skills (how to make decisions, evaluate alternatives, identify tension and conflict, negotiate, develop the will to find solutions)
  —What children have to say
  —How our social fabric is affected by a war economy and the rejection of social justice
  —Factors that create and maintain peace, security and social order.

One essay, "Children and the Threat of Nuclear War", discusses the particular difficulties of talking with kids about nuclear issues, how children cope with thoughts about nuclear dangers, and how parents can help their children at different ages. After reading it, take this book to your local school, PTA, and other groups.

Reweaving the Web of Life
  ed. by Pam McAllister; 1982; New Society Publishers, Philadelphia
Feminism and Non-Violence—An anthology of poems, essays, songs and observations that is charged with excitement, strength and vital inspiration. The many threads form an amazing tapestry—and a lifeline.

Protest and Survive
E.P. Thompson and Dan Smith; 1981; Monthly Review Press, New York

In 1980, public outrage over a British civil defense pamphlet "Protect and Survive" reinforced European demands for disarmament, and organized commitment to peace on the governmental level. One response was the publication of *Protest and Survive*. This American version includes: detailed and factual critiques of the official nuclear weapons policies of the U.K., U.S., NATO, the USSR, and Warsaw Pact countries; a good look at the world-wide military-industrial complex; an insider's description of what goes on at the Department of Defense; and proposals that emphasize the urgency of acting now.

Kiss Sleeping Beauty Good-Bye
Madonna Kolbenschlag; 1979; Bantam Books, New York

Involved in the details and demands of daily life, and without experience in considering alternatives, it can be difficult to understand our own contribution to situations we don't like. Using fairy tales as illustrations, Kolbenschlag examines some of the ways women support, and contribute to the violent and destructive aspects of our society.

A Manual on Non-Violence and Children
ed. by Stephanie Judson; 1984; New Society Publishers, Philadelphia

Skills, values, and concepts of peace are introduced through songs, games, conversations, and descriptions of actual situations. Five elements are emphasized: affirmation, sharing feelings and experience, creating a supportive community, problem-solving, and enjoying life. Written by teachers of young children, it is equally valuable in the home. An excellent bibliography of children's books is included.

The Cooperative Sports and Games Book
Terry Orlick; 1978; Pantheon, New York

Challenge without Competition—Watching children for a while reveals a vast difference between their natural play and the restricted types of games usually available to them. Orlick has broadened the options with a wonderful collection of over 100 games, both active and quiet, grouped for ages from three to adult. The emphasis is on keeping all players involved, and especially on *fun*!

For Children

The Story of Ferdinand
Munro Leaf; 1936; Viking Press, New York

Although intended for glory in the ring, and recognized by an adoring public as the strongest, "the largest and fiercest bull of all," Ferdinand sticks to his own priorities—"He liked to sit just quietly and smell the flowers." Children have loved this story for generations.

Swimmy

Leo Lionni; 1963; Random House, New York

Little fish get eaten by big fish—or do they? Not when the little fishes get together to take advantage of Swimmy's inspiration!

Half a Kingdom

Ann McGovern; 1978; Scholastic Book Services, New York

A clever and resourceful peasant girl uses an open mind and a down-to-earth approach at every step of an adventure that is more complicated than it looked at the start. The humor and beautiful pictures are especially nice elements for grownups, who will be asked to read it more than once.

Anansi the Spider

Gerald McDermott; 1977; Penguin Books, New York

In this famous African fairy tale, it takes the different abilities of all six sons of Anansi the Clever to get him out of trouble. Which one should be given the reward? Anansi gets help on that one, too.

Song of the Trees

Mildred Taylor; 1975; Dial Press, New York

Mr. Anderson is determined to get the lumber he wants from the Logan's cherished grove of trees. By his reckoning, he has the right to take it; he certainly has the position and power. But Mr. Logan knows there are many sources of authority, and that resistance can succeed, even when your opponent seems to hold all the cards.

The Peace Book

Bernard Benson; 1980; Bantam Books, New York

What if . . . a little boy used Gandhi's techniques of dialogue, creative resistance, and focusing attention on survival, in dealing with the governments of the superpowers? A new fairy tale.

The Little White Horse

Elizabeth Goudge; 1978; Scholastic Book Services, New York

Maria sets herself to resolving a long-standing quarrel among the residents of Moonacre Manor, originally caused by her ancestors. Helped by her human and animal friends, and sustained by Marmaduke Scarlet's veal pie, she eventually gets people unstuck from their old grievances.

For Adults

Small is Beautiful
E.F. Schumacher; 1981; Harper & Row, New York
The logic of our vast industrial and technical systems is being challenged by events. For 40 years, this noted British economist has been studying what can be done. He concludes that progress will come, not from more resources, but from their control and use on a human scale, and that the traditional wisdom of mankind has much to offer us in developing a society where the needs of people matter more than those of organizations.

The Turning Point
Fritjof Capra; 1982; Simon & Schuster, New York
Dr. Capra believes that under the pressure of the crises generated by our wastefulness, our sense of reality is changing. A view of 'facts' and 'the real world' which acknowledges that all actions are essentially related, and dependent on each other, is beginning to make it possible for our society to operate on the values of wholeness, balance and health.

Building a Sustainable Society
Lester R. Brown; 1981; W.W. Norton & Co., New York
"We have inherited the Earth from our parents; we are borrowing it from our children." The President of the Worldwatch Institute in Washington, DC describes the world-wide problems caused by using up natural resources—from topsoil to oil—and suggests ways of developing a less threatened society.

The Aquarian Conspiracy
Marilyn Ferguson; 1980; J.P. Tarcher, Los Angeles
Conspire literally means 'breathe together'; Aquarius, the Water Bearer, is the sign of the generous flow of life. During her years as a science reporter, the author noticed that the same words and concepts were being used by people in different scientific and professional fields. Using her background and 185 responses to an extensive questionnaire, she explains the actual discoveries that are being made, and how they are contributing to a new American perspective.

Green Paradise Lost
Elizabeth Dodson Gray; 1979; Roundtable Press, Wellesley, MA
Re-mything Genesis—Can we re-enter the world we live in? A basic introduction to biology, health, ecology, physics and culture, based on the assumption that the universe is a rhythm, not a machine. This scholar emphasizes that our social and physical existence depends on a living mesh, not a ladder of cause and effect.

Akwesasne Notes
> Mohawk Nation (via Trumansburg) NY 13683

A publication of the Mohawk Nation, put out by people in a unique position to understand our common dilemma. Both their traditional sense of self-reliance, which comes with the knowledge of belonging, and their long experience with the threat of extinction give Native Americans important expertise in dealing with today's problems. This lively journal contains news, articles, book reviews, interviews, etc. It's written from a perspective that accepts the power of harmony.

The Dispossessed
> Ursula K. Le Guin; 1975; Avon Books, New York

There are many kinds of mystery and adventure. For example: When a group of people have created a way of life they believe in, what happens then? And how can individuals with unique and special visions express themselves without being disloyal to their community, or threatening it? On the twin planets of Anarres and Urras, a physicist devotes himself to removing walls of custom and distrust in this famous saga of politics, love and desire.

Taking Charge
> by the Simple Living Collective of AFSC; 1977; Bantam Books, New York

Personal and Political Change through Simple Living—There are many possibilities for increasing our individual and general well-being. This down-to-earth manual covers: —Consuming Ourselves—Consuming the World—Personal Growth—Community—Children Taking Charge—Work—Creative Simplicity—Clothing—Health Care—Using Energy and Living Simply—The Energy Addict's Calorie Counter—Food—Another View of Economics.

Food

Well-nourished life, from plants to people, is more resistant to disease, pollution and other injury. Unfortunately, physical health and the economic health of the food industry have different requirements. Nutritional value is not an important factor in the growing, processing and packaging of the food we buy. But information is available that makes it possible to reduce the effects of modern agricultural technology on our personal well-being.

Laurel's Kitchen
> Laurel Robertson, Carol Flinders and Bronwen Godfrey; 1976; Bantam Books, New York

This cookbook begins with a long account of how the author's interest in food with more flavor has contributed to a gradual change in her outlook and habits. She shares what she's learned about meal planning, using unprocessed food, and techniques for preserving food's nutrients. As a young mother, she came to feel that avoiding meat was a way of giving life, and she's now a vegetarian. Using this book feels like learning to cook with a friend in her kitchen.

Diet for a Small Planet

Frances M. Lappé; 1975; Ballantine Books, New York

Concerned by world hunger, Lappé began to investigate our food supply. Shocked by the fact that the American agricultural system uses one-half our farm land and 100 pounds of plant protein to produce 10 pounds of meat protein, she thoroughly researched protein-rich, meat-free options. This information has particular importance for people today, since eating animal products now exposes us to increased health risks. Many radioactive and toxic chemicals—pesticides, industrial wastes, and other environmental contaminants—become more concentrated as they rise through food chains. (Plants are at the low end of food chains. They are eaten by animals. When we eat the animals, we're eating at the top of the food chains.) She includes not only recipes, but the practical charts, tables and cost comparisons she's used in her personal adventure: " . . . the discovery of ways, the best, most delicious ways, of making the most of the earth's productivity."

Nutrition Almanac

John Kirschmann; 1973; McGraw Hill, New York

An encyclopedic manual that covers all aspects of nutrition:

—Health
—Sources of calories, vitamins and minerals
—The composition of food
—Common ailments and stresses
—Herbs
—and more.

The Enchanted Broccoli Forest

Mollie Katzen; 1982; Ten Speed Press, Berkeley, CA

and Other Timeless Delicacies—Using the great traditional cuisines of the world, the author of "The Moosewood Cookbook" offers good food that's good for you. This collection includes a variety of plain and festive recipes—from enchiladas to blintzes, cookies to curried soups. A cookbook written by and for people who love food.

The Self-Sufficient Gardener

John Seymour; 1979; Dell Publishing Co., New York

A Complete Guide to Growing and Preserving All Your Own Food—It is less than a hundred years since Americans ate (as most people in the world still do) food grown in our gardens, or locally. Of course, 'raising your own' provides the now-rare luxury of really fresh food, and it can save you money; it also means being able to control what goes into and onto food we eat. The wonderful illustrations and clear explanations in this book cover everything from cycles and seasons to pests and planning. It's especially useful for people with limited space.

For Children

Thirteen

Remy Charlip and Jerry Joyner; 1974; Parent's Magazine Press, New York

In contrast to conventional books that go from page to page, and scene to scene, Charlip and Joyner have copied the real world by having lots of things going on at once. On each page, 13 beautiful picture stories, shows, and jokes develop in their own ways. For instance: "Swans Becoming Water", "A Perfect Day", and "Reflections of a Worm". Reading it is a wonderful adventure.

Frederick

Leon Lionni; 1966; Pantheon, New York

Frederick is a mouse who doesn't fit in. His brothers tease him and are resentful that he sits around watching the summer instead of doing his share or preparing for winter. But when the long winter is finally upon them, they discover that his unnoticed talents are also necessary for their survival.

Jo, Flo, and Yolanda

Carol de Poix; 1973; Lollipop Power, Chapel Hill, NC

Jo, Flo and Yolanda are triplets. They are close, but different. They look alike, but not quite the same. Some things they like to do together, but each one has individual interest. They are all part of the same hard-working, loving family. A simple story that helps children feel safe.

How to Care for Your Monster

Norman Bridwell; 1972; Scholastic Book Services, New York

A useful book no child should be without. It lists the most popular monsters, describes their care and feeding, and helps you decide which one is most appropriate for *you*. ("If your family is always telling you to turn down the record player, and not to shout, giggle, or slam doors, then choose a mummy. He makes very little noise . . . ") Tips on buying or catching them are included.

Wheel on the School

Meindert De Jong; 1954; Harper & Row, New York

One of the six school children in a small Dutch village writes what she knows about storks. They nest in the area, why not in Shora? The teacher asks them to think about it. "For sometimes when we wonder, we can make things begin to happen." Bringing back the storks becomes the children's dream, and as they search for one nesting wheel, the whole community, from very old to very young, becomes involved. We follow them through discouragement, setbacks that lead to unsuspected possibilities, and adventures along the way. New relationships are formed, crucial help comes from people who seem to have nothing to offer. By the time they find out their dream can come true, many things have changed.

Cockleburr Quarters

Charlotte Baker; 1972; Avon Books, New York

Mrs. Randall sets great store by the parable of the leaven—the little bit of yeast that turns flour and water into bread. Dolph doesn't understand until his love for a half-blind stray and her puppies involves him in the work, joy and pain of caring; the reversed, inevitable mistakes and successes of trying—and the effects of his commitment spread through the neighborhood. Suddenly, decisions he can't influence change everything. "The world is a lump, all right, thought Dolph. Big and heavy enough to weigh me down forever. Make it lighter? Make it rise? No way. No way." But Dolph is resilient and has gained confidence in his power to make unlikely things happen.

The Sword in the Stone

T.H. White; 1939; Dell Publishing Co., New York

Wart manages to be reasonably happy in spite of being a foster brother who's picked on by the real son of the manor. When the boys get a tutor who's a magician, life really begins to look up. The magician feels that turning Wart into various animals is an essential part of his education. Dragons, a giant, and knights in rusty armor add excitement to this delightful and detailed tale of life in medieval England.

A Ring of Endless Light

Madeline L'Engle; 1980; Dell Publishing Co., New York

Her conviction that reality, however terrible, is better than "plastic pretense" is tested during the summer Vicky Austin and her family spend with Vicky's beloved and dying grandfather. At the same time, she's involved with 3 very different boys: Zachary offers the thrill of wealth and danger; Leo, the solidity of loyal friendship; Adam, the challenge of partnership and intimate communication. But ultimately, it's the wild dolphins she gets to know who give her the perspective necessary to accept death and loss, and the joy of living.

Organizations

There are hundreds of groups and organizations working for peace and environmental safety. Most of the organizations listed below are national centers which will send out information on request, and direct you to their local affiliate.

FOE (Friends of the Earth)
124 Spears St.
San Francisco, CA 94105

NIRS (Nuclear Information and Resource Service)
1346 Connecticut Ave. NW
Washington, DC 20036

WISE (World Information Service on Energy)
1536 16th St., NW
Washington, DC 20036

•In the Three Mile Island area:

TMI Public Interest Resource Center
1037 Maclay St.
Harrisburg, PA 17103

Concerned Mothers
c/o Paula Kinney
12 Ray Road
Middletown, PA 17057

No Nukes!

AFSC (American Friends Service Committee)
1501 Cherry St.
Philadelphia, PA 19102

Business Alert to Nuclear War
Box 7
Belmont, MA 02178

Council for a Livable World
100 Maryland Ave. NE
Washington, DC 20002

Ground Zero
Room 421
806 15th St. NW
Washington, DC 20002

Jobs with Peace National Network
2940 16th St., Rm B-1
San Francisco, CA 94103

MNS (Movement for a New Society)
4722 Baltimore Ave.
Philadelphia, PA 19143

MFS Mobilization for Survival
48 Marks Pl.
New York, NY 10003

NARMIC (National Action/Research on the Military-Industrial Complex)
1501 Cherry St.
Philadelphia, PA 19102

PSR (Physicians for Social Responsibility)
25 Main St.
P.O. Box 144
Watertown, MA 02172

SANE (Committee for a Sane Nuclear Policy)
318 Massachusetts Ave. NE
Washington, DC 20002

Toward Peace

Traprock Peace Center
Keats Road
Deerfield, MA 01342

USC Union of Concerned
Scientists)
1384 Massachusetts Ave.
Cambridge, MA 02138

WAND (Women's Action for
Nuclear Disarmament, Inc.)
P.O. Box 153
New Town Branch
Boston, MA 02258

WILPF (Women's International
League for Peace and Freedom)
1213 Race St.
Philadelphia, PA 19107

WPA (Women's Pentagon Action)
339 Lafayette Ave.
New York, NY 10012

WSP (Women Strike for Peace)
145 South 13th St., Rm 407
Philadelphia, PA 19107

Environmental Alternatives

Center for Science in the Public Interest
1755 S St. NW
Washington, DC 20009

CEP (Citizen's Energy Project)
1413 K St. NW
8th Floor
Washington, DC 20005

FREE (Feminist Resources in Energy and Ecology)
Box 6098, Teall Station
Syracuse, NY 13217

Greenpeace
2007 R St. NW
Washington, DC 20009

NCAT (National Center for Appropriate Technology)
P.O. Box 3838
Butte, MT 59701

NEATN (Northeast Appropriate Technology Network)
P.O. Box 548
Greenfield, MA 01301

PIRG (Public Interest Research Group)
1346 Connecticut Ave. NW
Washington, DC 20036

Solar Lobby
1001 Connecticut Ave., NW
Washington, DC 20036

Children, Parents, and Teachers

ACT (Action for Children's Television)
46 Austin St.
Newtonville, MA 02160

CCND (Children's Campaign for Nuclear Disarmament)
14 Everit St.
New Haven, CT 06511

CCRC (Children's Creative Response to Conflict)
Box 271
Nyack, NJ 10960

CEASE (Concerned Educators Allied for a Safe Environment)
18618 Manzanita Road
Sonoma, CA 95476
(West of the Mississippi)

17 Gerry St.
Cambridge, MA 02138
(East of the Mississippi)

COPRED (Consortium on Peace Research, Education and Development)
Kent State University
Kent, OH 44242

ESR (Educators for Social Responsibility)
23 Garden St.
Cambridge, MA 02138

Grandmothers for Peace
2708 Curtis Way
Sacto, CA 95818

Interhelp
c/o Glide Church
330 Ellis Street
room 505
San Francisco, CA 94102

National Parenting for Peace and Justice
c/o Institute for Peace and Justice
4144 Lindell Blvd., # 400
St. Louis, MO 63108

NEP (Nuclear Education Project)
P.O. Box31
Somerville, MA 02144

Parenting in the Nuclear Age
c/o 6501 Telegraph Ave.
Oakland, CA 94609

PTSR (Parents and Teachers for Social Responsibility)
Box 517
Moretown, VT 05660

STOP (Student/Teacher Organization to Prevent Nuclear War)
Box 232
Northfield, MA 01360

Resources From New Society Publishers

"This is the bravest book I have read since Jonathan Schell's FATE OF THE EARTH."
— *Dr. Rollo May*

DESPAIR AND PERSONAL POWER IN THE NUCLEAR AGE
by Joanna Rogers Macy

Despair and Personal Power in the Nuclear Age is the first major book to examine our psychological responses to planetary perils and to lay the theoretical foundations for an empowering, personally-centered approach to social change. Included are sections on awakening in the nuclear age, relating to children and young people, guided meditations, empowerment rituals, and a special section on "Spiritual Exercises for a Time of Apocalypse." As described and excerpted in *New Age Journal* and *Fellowship Magazine*. Recommended for public libraries by *Library Journal*; selected for inclusion in the 1984 Women's Reading Program, General Board of Global Ministries, United Methodist Church.

200 pages. Appendices, resource lists, exercises. 1983.
Hardcover: $19.95
Paperback: $8.95

A MANUAL ON NONVIOLENCE AND CHILDREN
compiled and edited by Stephanie Judson;
Foreword by Paula J. Paul,
Educators for Social Responsibility

Includes "For the Fun of It! Selected Cooperative Games for Children and Adults"

Invaluable resource for creating an atmosphere in which children and adults can resolve problems and conflicts nonviolently. Especially useful for parents and teachers in instilling values today to create the peacemakers of tomorrow!

"Stephanie Judson's excellent manual has helped many parents and teachers with whom we have worked. An essential part of learning nonviolent ways of resolving conflicts is the creation of a trusting, affirming and cooperative environment in the home and classroom. This manual has a wealth of suggestions for creating such an environment. We highly recommend it."
—Jim and Kathy McGinnis,
Parenting for Peace and Justice,
St. Louis, Missouri

Anecdotes, exercises, games, agendas, annotated bibliography. Illustrated, large format. 160 pages. 1984.
Hardcover: $24.95
Paperback: $9.95

To Order:
send check or money order to
New Society Publishers
4722 Baltimore Avenue
Philadelphia, PA 19143
for postage and handling:
add $1.50 for the first book
and 40¢ for each additional book.

320 pages. 1984.
Hardcover: $24.95
Paperback: $10.95

WE ARE ALL PART OF ONE ANOTHER:
A BARBARA DEMING READER

*I have had the dream
that women should at last
be the ones to truly experiment
with nonviolent struggle,
discover its full force.*

Essays, speeches, letters, stories, poems by America's foremost writer on issues of women and peace, feminism and nonviolence, spanning four decades. Lovingly edited by activist-writer Jane Meyerding; Black feminist writer Barbara Smith, founder of Kitchen Table Press, has graciously contributed a foreword. A book no activist of the '80s will want to be without!

"Barbara Deming is the voice of conscience for her generation and all those to follow, measured in reason, compassionate, clear, requiring: the voice of a friend."   —Jane Rule

"Wisdom, modesty, responsiveness, love: all of these qualities live in her writings, a treasured gift to the world."   —Leah Fritz

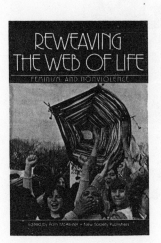

448 pages.
Hardcover: $19.95
Paperback: $10.95

To Order:
send check or money order to
New Society Publishers
4722 Baltimore Avenue
Philadelphia, PA 19143
for postage and handling:
add $1.50 for the first book
and 40¢ for each additional book.

REWEAVING THE WEB OF LIFE:
FEMINISM AND NONVIOLENCE
edited by Pam McAllister

". . . happens to be one of the most important books you'll ever read."   —*The Village Voice*

"Stressing the connection between patriarchy and war, sex and violence, this book makes it clear that nonviolence can be an assertive, positive force. It's provocative reading for anyone interested in surviving and changing the nuclear age."

—*Ms. Magazine*

More than 50 Contributors – Women's History – Women and the Struggle Against Militarism – Violence and Its Origins – Nonviolence and Women's Self-Defense – Interviews – Songs – Poems – Stories – Provocative Proposals – Photographs – Annotated Bibliography – Index

Voted "Best New Book—1983"—*WIN MAGAZINE ANNUAL BOOK POLL*

GANDHI THROUGH WESTERN EYES
by Horace Alexander

"This book stands out as an authoritative guide: clear, simple, and straightforward, both to Gandhi's personality and to his beliefs. As a Quaker, Mr. Alexander found it easy to grasp Gandhi's ideas about nonviolence; the author's prolonged and intimate friendship helped him to know the Mahatma as few men were able to do, and to appreciate that he was something far greater than a national hero of the Indian independence movement—a man, in fact, with a message that is intensely relevant for the world today. Nothing that has so far been published about Gandhi is more illuminating than this careful, perceptive and comprehensive work. It is not only comprehensive—it is convincing."

—Times Literary Supplement

Letter, Index. 240 pages. 1984.
Hardcover: $24.95
Paperback: $8.95

NO TURNING BACK: LESBIAN AND GAY LIBERATION FOR THE '80s
by Gerre Goodman, George Lakey, Judy Lashof & Erika Thorne; Foreword by Malcolm Boyd

"*No Turning Back* fulfills a long felt need for a progressive analysis and pragmatic sourcebook for lesbians, gays and others concerned with replacing patriarchal oppression with a more human alternative. I was quite pleased by the integration of personal statements and experiences into the more theoretical discussion, and by the inclusion of practical and feasible proposals for individual and collective action."

> —Larry Gross, Professor, Annenberg School
> of Communications, University of Pennsylvania,
> and Co-Chair, Philadelphia Lesbian
> and Gay Task Force

Recommended for public libraries by *Library Journal.*

168 pages.
Hardcover: $16.95
Paperback: $7.95

WOMEN IN DEVELOPMENT: A RESOURCE GUIDE FOR ORGANIZATION AND ACTION
by ISIS Womens International Information and Communication Service.

A lavishly illustrated book, with 122 photographs, five years in the making. Women scholars from all over the world contributed to make this one of the most comprehensive and beautiful books of its kind ever published. Sections on women and multinationals, women and rural development, women and health, education, tourism, migration, etc.

Annotated resource lists, bibliographies.
240 pages. 1984.
Hardcover: $39.95
Paperback: $14.95

MORE THAN THE TROUBLES: A COMMON SENSE VIEW OF THE NORTHERN IRELAND CONFLICT

by Lynne Shivers and David Bowman, S.J.; foreword by Denis Barritt; afterword by Joseph Fahey, S.J. on "Northern Ireland: Its Relevance for Peace Education."

"No stereotypes about Northern Ireland and its people, its religion, or politics can survive a reading of this carefully constructed account of a packed and eventful history where past and future compete for attention in the present. The juxtaposition of bitter conflict and cooperation makes this story a microcosm of the human condition in this century. The difficult task of documentation is done with loving care. As readers we are at once humbled, sobered, and inspired. . . ."

> —Dr. Elise Boulding, Professor of Sociology, Dartmouth College and the University of Colorado; founder of COPRED (Consortium on Peace Reseach, Education and Development)

Index, appendices, maps, charts, bibliography, photographs.
240 pages. 1984.
Hardcover: $24.95

THE EYE OF THE CHILD

by Ruth Mueller

A brilliant healing myth for a world gone mad!

"Of all the creatures to whom the great mother had given birth all were a part, not apart, but one. Yes all but one flowed as she flowed, born of her womb, dying in her bosom, struggling, true, but never against their own life support. One, only one, capable of standing apart, imagining self above and outside, turning to rend, turning to overpower, to subdue, to conquer the vessel of life itself, creation's own embodiment. Had she not labored for aeons to give birth to a triumph of joy and beauty as fair as dawn, a creature of light to share the glowing consciousness of the whole, one of understanding as deep as her deeps are deep, of laughter as divine as tears and of tears as cleansing as laughter, one who was no alien to mercy, capable of new visions above predation, a familiar to the art of healing, above all a creature of tongues, creation itself no longer mute to express—to express—

"What had gone wrong?"

Ecological speculative fiction of the highest order.

240 pages. 1984.
Paperback: $7.95

To Order:
send check or money order to
New Society Publishers
4722 Baltimore Avenue
Philadelphia, PA 19143
for postage and handling:
add $1.50 for the first book
and 40¢ for each additional book.